6-30-98

For Jeff –

With our best w

Anne & Niki McC

Selling Strategies for Today's Banker

Selling Strategies
for
Today's
Banker

A Survival Guide
for Tomorrow

**Dennis McCuistion, CSP &
Niki Nicastro McCuistion, CSP**

Dearborn
Financial Publishing, Inc.

While a great deal of care has been taken to provide accurate and current information, the ideas, suggestions, general principles and conclusions presented in this text are subject to local, state and federal laws and regulations, court cases and any revisions of same. The reader is thus urged to consult legal counsel regarding any points of law—this publication should not be used as a substitute for competent legal advice.

Publisher: Kathleen A. Welton
Associate Editor: Karen A. Christensen
Senior Project Editor: Jack L. Kiburz
Cover and Interior Design: Lucy Jenkins

Published by Dearborn Financial Publishing, Inc.

Printed in the United States of America

91 92 93   10 9 8 7 6 5 4 3 2 1

Library of Congress Cataloging-in-Publication Data

McCuistion, Dennis.
    Selling strategies for today's banker: a survival guide for
tomorrow/Dennis McCuistion, Niki Nicastro McCuistion.
        p.   cm.
    Includes bibliographical references and index.
    ISBN 0-79310-212-X
    1. Selling—Banks and banking. 2. Bank management—United
States. I. McCuistion, Niki Nicastro. II. Title.
HF5439.B35M33   1991   91–26941
332.1'2'0688—dc20   CIP

Table of Contents

Preface

Change and *sell* are two very hard words for bankers to accept. And yet, there is no choice about either. The only choice we have is to accept and deal proactively with both or be pulled kicking and screaming into acceptance. We advocate the former.

This book is for bankers and other financial service providers. The subject is selling—what it is, why it's essential in today's environment, why bankers resist it and, most especially, how to sell and enjoy it. We wrote the book primarily for community bankers though the principles hold true for banks of any size. Larger banks are already heavily involved in selling and many have made the change to a sales culture. Banks with $500 million in assets and below usually cannot afford hundreds of thousands of dollars for training and advice. This book is for you.

We believe that today's bankers, to survive and thrive in the future, must create a sales culture which so permeates the entire organization that customers are amazed at the level of service they receive. In a time of employee layoffs, mergers and bank closings, too many banks have merely cut back; morale, not to mention customer responsiveness, has suffered.

Writing this book was not easy. One of us is a career banker and bank consultant; the other is a sales and marketing consultant. We lead seminars and speak to bankers all over the country. The salesperson had to convince the banker why selling was not "offensive" and could be done with integrity. She succeeded, but not without difficulty. He kept insisting, "But bankers are bankers because they don't want to sell." Oh, there were all kinds of objections to selling that led to what we refer to as the banker's mind-set. Somehow we had to overcome an inherent negativity about selling before we could teach bankers how to do it.

In effect, we decided to analyze precisely why bankers don't want to sell, then identify why bankers must sell, before we showed how to sell with integrity while increasing the bottom line. So we decided to survey thousands of our seminar participants and several of our friends and clients in this business. And were we amazed at what we found! In the book you'll see our survey form and its results. In particular, Chapter 14 contains over 75 of the best ideas that bankers shared with us—ideas that have worked for their banks, ideas that you, the reader, may be able to adopt for your own use. Our belief is that bankers are more likely to adopt programs that other bankers have used successfully rather than create programs from scratch.

There are two other unique features of this book. One is the premise that we've used throughout—that "selling" in a bank is actually "helping." But, interestingly, most bankers have never thought of selling that way. We believe that this concept is the secret to overcoming a banker's natural skepticism about selling.

The other unique feature is covered in separate chapters telling how the sales process affects five distinct areas of the bank:

1. The board of directors
2. The CEO
3. Managers, supervisors and lenders
4. Customer contact personnel
5. Back office personnel

After we define the problem in Chapters 1 and 2 and teach you how to sell in Chapters 3 through 7, we devote one chapter to each of the five groups. In Chapter 14 our survey ideas are also organized in a similar manner. Chapter 13 pulls it all together and discusses the importance of relationships with customers. The final chapter provides information on sales from other sources.

We recommend that you read through the entire book first. Then go back over the parts that apply specifically to your own areas of responsibility. This book can provide the framework for an easy-to-use, cost-effective, in-house training program. We wrote the book to "help" you because we truly believe that is what banking is all about.

We couldn't have written it without the incredible people who attend our seminars and share their ideas, and the people we talk to at banking associations around the country. We thank our past and present clients, with special thanks to those who took their valuable time to read this and give us feedback. We appreciate Ralph McCalmont of BancFirst in Oklahoma and Robert D. Dye of Gary-Wheaton Bank in Illinois. And, of course, our diligent office staff who labored over the manuscript—especially Sandi Mitchell.

Thanks to our terrific agent, Jeff Herman, in New York and our editor at Dearborn, Kathy Welton. We appreciate your confidence, support, assistance and, yes, patience.

Finally, we want to thank each other for being partner, spouse and best friend—and especially for remaining so throughout the process of writing this book.

Dennis McCuistion, CSP
Niki Nicastro McCuistion, CSP

CHAPTER 1

Selling: Its Problems and Challenges

"How many of you *like* to sell?" is one of two key questions that we have asked thousands of bank, credit union and savings and loan employees in our seminars over the past five years. In general, even in the early 1990s, there will be a *minimum* of five hands to a *maximum* of 15 in every audience of 100. That's right—only 5 to 15 percent of you like to sell! Is it any wonder that so many in the financial services industry are ineffective when it comes to selling?

How many things in your life do you do well that you don't *like* to do? Are you likely to be a great golfer if you hate the game? Will you be a great bridge player if you don't like card games? Are you likely to be a good accountant if you don't like numbers? The answer to these questions is obvious, and many of you are undoubtedly thinking what we've heard many times before: "One of the reasons I got into banking was so that I wouldn't have to *sell* something." Well, you're not alone. The vast majority of bankers feel that way. And yet, virtually every banker we've surveyed agrees that the ability to sell is critical if you are to succeed in this business. There is no choice.

Many readers will not finish reading this book for a variety of reasons. Part of our task is to provide a way for you the reader to become self-motivated.

OUR PLEDGE TO YOU

If you read, study and apply the principles and ideas in this book, we promise that you will get at least the following benefits:

1. You will be able to provide a significantly higher quality of service to your present customers.
2. You will be able, if you choose to do so, to actually call on and recruit new customer business without undergoing a life-changing experience.
3. You will gain a broader understanding of the importance of your job.
4. You will become a more valuable team player, which may lead to increased responsibilities and increased pay.

WHAT DO WE WANT FROM YOU?

First, we want you to read this book from start to finish and mark those points that are especially important from your present perspective.

Second, we ask that you carefully review the most important points and arrive at your own personal action plan. We ask that you then share your plans with your coworkers and *set deadlines* that will encourage you to follow through. Finally, we ask that you *record* at least some of your successes based on your new perspectives and action plans.

It has been demonstrated that merely reading a book will not change a person's behavior. Only through a behavioral change can you achieve the promised benefits. Such a change must take place over time, while you are carrying out your action plans.

WHAT'S THE PROBLEM?

Why is there such an emphasis on sales and marketing in to-day's financial services industry? What has caused these changes? We'll go into the answers in depth in Chapter 2. For now, just remember this:

■ ■ ■

Banks are losing their market share to other financial services providers.

■ ■ ■

The combinations of factors that have caused banks to lose their market share to other financial services providers include the following:

- Inflation and other government-induced market uncertainties
- New and aggressive competition
- Deregulation and other structural industry changes
- Tax policies
- Technology

FROM THE CONSERVATIVE TO THE CHAOTIC

If there is one word that describes banking over the past 20 years, most assuredly that word is *change*. But—and here's the secret—that same word describes almost every activity and business as well. We see change so well in banking because it personally affects us in this industry.

Bankers have historically been blessed with all or a part of a mind-set that includes four major beliefs:

1. We have products and services that are "different" and scarce, and our role is to ration them properly among those who want them.
2. Salespeople are unprofessional and pushy, as personified by the offensive used-car salesman; therefore, selling is something we consciously and subconsciously do not want to do.
3. We can provide additional services to our customers if we can get the legislative and regulatory approval to provide

such services and products as insurance, real estate, securities, etc.

4. We have a long-term, special relationship with our customers, and our desire is to enhance that relationship and attract new customers to a similar relationship.

Can you identify with this mind-set? Do you, or did you, share these beliefs? To a greater or lesser extent, some of them still hold true. Let's briefly examine each.

1. Do we offer unique products and services today? Or, isn't it true that the products and services we offer are pretty much the same as those of our competition? If this is so, then doesn't it follow that *how* the products and services are offered is perhaps more important than *which* products and services are offered?

2. Yes, many salespeople are pushy and obnoxious. But are they the ones you like to deal with? Think about why you buy from one supplier and not another. Is it partially due to price and convenience? Perhaps. But in your most intimate service relationships (and what is more intimate than money?) don't you look for something more? Aren't you looking for someone who is willing and able to *help* you? If you fail to remember anything else about this book, please remember this:

■ ■ ■

Sell is a four-letter word. So is *help*. We want you to mentally substitute the word *help* for *sell* each time you see it in this book and elsewhere.

■ ■ ■

We believe that people stay in the banking business for one major reason: they like to help people. By studying these ideas you can help your customer better than ever before. Surely, that is not difficult to do.

3. We want to encourage you to actively support your American Bankers Association and your state associations that are working to gain additional service capabilities. Many of your competitors offer a full complement of services.

Can you blame customers for taking their savings accounts to a brokerage firm that also handles securities and makes loans? And, what about that competition? Do they have the old, conservative non-selling banker mentality? Hardly. They are salespeople first, and money experts second.

4. We believe in relationships, and so do you. Repeat business is like an annuity—it just keeps paying off. In this book, we intend to show you step-by-step methods that will not only help you form a new relationship, but, more importantly, build and cement your present ones. Most of your new business will come from your present customers. Are you afraid to help them? We think not. And this book will assist you in overcoming the natural reluctance you may have to selling.

DEFINING OUR TERMS

It is important to understand specifically what is meant by several very important terms. Here we are providing you with the definitions we prefer. We hope you'll agree that they are simple, yet powerful.

Marketing is finding out what the customer wants, and delivering the product or service at a price the customer will pay, at a place and in a manner the customer chooses.

Marketing at its best is not inventing a product and pushing it on unsuspecting customers. It is finding out what the customers want and then devising a product to meet that need. Marketing is viewing your business from the customer's point of view. Can you see how much easier it is to accomplish the sale if the product is already desired?

Selling is that part of the marketing process wherein the buyer's specific needs are identified, the product or service is offered, and commitment from the customer is gained. If done correctly, selling is no more than helping customers achieve their own goals while enhancing bank goals as well.

We will lead you through a step-by-step process beginning in Chapter 3 that will enable you to help your customers in a manner that greatly enhances both relationships and profitability.

Consultative selling is a proven system that builds agreement with your customers throughout the sales process by focusing on their needs and concerns.

By identifying their needs and offering the bank/financial solution that is right for them, you earn referrals and build toward long-term relationships. The relationship you have built makes getting commitment a matter of *when,* not *if.*

Market share is your share of present deposits, assets or loan volume that your bank controls compared to other financial institutions in your market. Growth for its own sake is passé for banks of the 1990s; however, leaders in market share do hold some comparative competitive market advantages, which can translate to bottom line profits.

Competition is any other institution that offers all or a part of the products or services offered by your bank.

Competition today includes government (both direct and indirect through various agencies and quasi-government entities), other banks and savings and loans, finance companies, credit unions, department store and other charge cards, brokerage and insurance companies, and perhaps many more. A constant reassessment of what others are doing to meet customer needs is an integral part of marketing and sales strategy.

Customer-driven refers to a marketing strategy in which virtually all products and services are formulated to meet customer wants, and services and products are delivered in a manner of unexcelled performance.

Dozens of our surveys that bankers completed to help us write this book contained words to this effect: "We strive to provide the best [or most excellent] customer service." And that's as expected. But when we say customer-driven, we want you to think of service delivered in such a consistently passionate and superior way that your own customers become your best salespeople.

Sales culture is a feeling within an organization led from the top that permeates the entire staff with a passion for helping customers.

Don't confuse this with sloppy credit work or putting everyone on an incentive program to bring in large CDs. A sales culture simply means that the board and top management have recognized that achieving McCuistion's axiom is the prime business of the bank:

■ ■ ■

Getting and keeping the customer is the single most important skill a banker can develop.

■ ■ ■

HOW TO GET THE MOST FROM THIS BOOK

In considering the most effective way to communicate selling strategies, we have segmented our information in two major ways:

First, specific parts of this book will be aimed at five separate functional areas of the bank:

1. The board of directors
2. The CEO
3. Managers, supervisors and loan officers
4. Customer contact personnel
5. Back office personnel

While we firmly believe in a coordinated marketing/sales approach implemented from the top down, we also see specific suggestions being more or less relevant to specific groups. Thus, you will find that many of our comments are directed primarily at one or more of the above groups. We want you to read all of them the first time through, then go back and concentrate on those that specifically relate to *your* area of influence.

Someone once said, "Nothing breeds success like success." With this idea in mind, we began a research process in 1988 wherein we asked thousands of bankers to share their success-ful strategies with us. We wish we had room in this book for all of them, but we've had to choose those most relevant to the points we're trying to emphasize.

Second, vignettes are liberally sprinkled throughout the book and in a closing appendix. Our belief is that bankers can best implement products and provide service if they can be shown how such programs are being successfully used else-where. A word of caution: No single bank can or should try to implement all of these ideas. Just select a few that, based on *your* market research and personnel, will work for you.

The Chinese character for the word *crisis* consists of two parts: one part denotes danger, the other, opportunity. The decade of the 1980s certainly presented bankers with a clear and present danger. About 1,000 banks in existence prior to 1980 have now disappeared. Mergers have eliminated even more. But the true danger in the future is that our inability to provide new and innovative ways to keep customers will cause even more banks to fail or be swallowed up by default. The trend toward increasing government ownership can only lead to poorer service and frustration on the part of our customers. But the good news is that a bank whose personnel are thor-oughly trained and customer-driven will have even more op-portunities to prosper and profit in the Nineties.

SUMMARY

Bankers in the Nineties find themselves on the proverbial horns of a dilemma. On the one hand we generally don't like to sell. On the other, we all recognize the need to do so. Banks are losing market share due to inflation, competition, deregula-tion and technology, and to regain previous levels of perform-ance they must make changes.

Bankers have operated under a mind-set that is now suspect.

But instead of changing your mind-set, we've chosen to re-define "selling" as "helping" and to concentrate on present strengths: keeping and building relationships.

CHAPTER 2

Why Aren't Bankers More Sales-Oriented?

"Everyone tends to have tunnel vision and becomes so involved with their job that they tend not to think of the customer."

"We are not totally aware of what the product mix is and what it can do for the customer."

"There are not enough good training programs."

"Many people went to work in banks because they didn't want to be salesmen. They wanted to have the customer come to them and didn't want to be commissioned."

"We are often motivated by a lack of training and fear of rejection."

    The above comments are just a few of hundreds we've received from bankers all over the country. We asked bankers to complete a survey that included the questions shown in Figure 2.1. This chapter will examine why bankers should be sales-oriented—and why they're not.

FIGURE 2.1 **Executive Survey**

EXECUTIVE SURVEY

We are doing research for a book we're writing on the need for marketing and sales skills in the financial institution of the future. Your help in this effort would be appreciated. Please complete both sides of this form.

1. In your opinion, is there a need for Directors, Officers and Employees of financial institutions to improve their marketing/sales skills?   **Yes ☐   No ☐**

    If yes, why?

    _____

    _____

    _____

2. In your opinion, why is it difficult for financial institution employees to be marketing-oriented?

    _____

    _____

    _____

3. If you had cost-effective, easy-to-use, basic materials, what benefits would you expect to receive from having used these materials?

    _____

    _____

    _____

FIGURE 2.1   Executive Survey (continued)

4. Who within the organization should be trained in being more marketing oriented? Check all that apply.

    ☐ Directors   ☐ New Accounts Personnel

    ☐ CEO   ☐ Tellers
    ☐ Loan Officers   ☐ Others (Please Specify):_____

    ☐ Calling Account Officers   _____

5. Would *your* institution have an interest in a method to enhance customer referrals from your regular and advisory board members?   **Yes** ☐ **No** ☐

6. Which of the following materials would your organization be likely to use? Please rank (1), (2), (3) with (1) being the most likely to be used.

    ☐ Book ☐ Audio Cassettes ☐ Video Cassettes

7. Please indicate the *maximum* amount that you would be willing to pay for the previously listed materials.

Book	**Audio Cassettes**	**Video Cassettes**
☐ $20.00	☐ $50.00	☐ $ 50.00
☐ $40.00	☐ $60.00	☐ $ 75.00
☐ $50.00	☐ $75.00	☐ $125.00
		☐ $150.00
		☐ $195.00

8. One of the key components in our research is being able to "share the good news." In other words, instead of telling so many "war stories" about how we made bad loan decisions, it is much more positive to be able to say, "This is how the Second National Bank managed to capture new customers, increase profits, become sales oriented, utilize directors in marketing, etc.!"

FIGURE 2.1   **Executive Survey (continued)**

If you have a success story, however small or large, won't you share it with us and give us permission to use it in our book or other training materials? You may use the space below to describe your program or attach another sheet or two or enclose newspaper articles and other handouts. **Don't be modest!**

_____

_____

_____

_____

_____

_____

Permission is granted to quote me in your books or training materials.

Name _____

Employer _____

Position _____

Address _____

_____

Phone _____

Please Return To: McCuistion & Associates, 601 San Juan Court, Irving, Texas 75062, (214) 717-0090

WHY SHOULD BANKERS SELL?

The Bank Marketing Association employed a team of Texas A&M University researchers in 1983. The results of their research were published in *Bankers Who Sell: Improving Selling Effectiveness In Banking*. Using a comprehensive questionnaire, they received 714 responses from both "retail" and "wholesale" banks. In-depth interviews were conducted at ten banks.

In a 1988 follow-up survey, *Selling in Banking: Today's Reality, Tomorrow's Opportunity*, Leonard Berry and Donna Massey Kantak reported that little had changed since 1983. In their 1988 work, Berry and Kantak noted three key reasons why selling skills are vital to bankers in the Nineties.

Competition. No one in banking has missed the impact of the changing nature of competition since partial deregulation in the early 1980s. While savings institutions have not been as competitive as expected due to the savings and loan crisis, it is still true that they, along with credit card companies, brokerage companies, credit unions and others, were already ahead of banking in the development of a sales culture. Bankers had, and have, some catching up to do.

New products and services. Many bankers we've interviewed have expressed their dismay with comments such as, "Not *another* new product, I haven't learned the last one yet."

Yes, many banks today are offering insurance products and packaged accounts to consumers, various cash management services to businesses, and financial planning and trust services to a variety of customers.

Relationship banking. A major emphasis in banking for the last 40 years has been on relationships. We remember well how community bankers in particular routinely used this approach: "Now Joe, you understand that we want all your business. Your checking accounts, savings accounts, car loans, vacation loans. And, look, if you have any relatives who need a safe place to keep their money, you bring it here, too. And remember, when your kid gets old enough to buy a car, well you know we'll finance it—so long as you guarantee it, Joe."

And 20 to 30 years ago, this approach worked well. In the 1980s, though, the competitive environment changed with new laws and the phasing out of Regulation Q. Bankers recognize today that more and more customers will switch banks for a quarter of a point. In short, customer loyalty is not what it once was. It is common knowledge that the more services a customer uses, the less likely he is to change banks. How do you get customers to use more services? You "help" them, of course.

In addition to the previous three reasons illustrating that selling skills are vital to bankers, here are several responses to our survey question, "Is there a need for directors, officers and employees of financial institutions to improve their marketing/ sales skills? If so, why?"

Virtually every answer to the first part of the question was "yes." Here are responses from a few bankers.

"Competition dictates this for survival! It's that simple."

LOGAN B. MANATT, Assistant Cashier
First Bank
Port Isabel, Texas

"Service is becoming one of the most important factors of doing business—especially community banks."

DENNIS VAUGHT, Vice President
Peoples Bank
Paint Lick, Kentucky

"...cross-selling is the only way to stay in business."

SUSAN FOOSE, Assistant Vice President
Canandaigua National Bank
Canandaigua, New York

"People do not want to sell."

CHARLES P. WILSON, President
McKenzie Banking Co.
McKenzie, Tennessee

"Because directors have *influence*, officers have *access* and employees have *contact* with the targeted market. Individually, they do fine. Combined, they are unbeatable."

> BILL CALHOUN, Vice Chairman
> Unity National Bank
> Houston, Texas

IS IT DIFFICULT FOR BANKERS TO BE MARKETING-ORIENTED?

This second survey question yielded answers that were expected—and some that were not. Here's a sample.

"In the past we never had to. Even in deregulation the other 'financial institutions,' e.g., Sears, were not a factor in our area. Training is still not sales-oriented. A bank served people. A teller counted money, did not engage in cross-selling. [Marketing]...still goes against the grain of the nature of banking in the past."

> MARK ESTES, Senior Vice President
> West Texas State Bank
> Snyder, Texas

"They haven't been programmed to do it. It's not their job. It isn't mentioned when they're hired."

> WAYNE M. TURNER, Senior Vice President
> First Commercial Bank
> Bradenton, Florida

"We have to be skeptical to a certain extent for loan quality. A marketing person seems to be more pro-customer."

> SHERON THORN, Assistant Vice President
> Southland Bank
> Dothan, Alabama

"We have more than enough to do in the office."

> MARK NOBLE, Account Representative
> CO Bank, Columbia, South Carolina

"Lack of proper motivation and training."

> WALTER McCRARY, JR., President
> First State Bank of Randolph County
> Cuthbert, Georgia

"Everyone tends to have tunnel vision and become so involved with their job they tend not to think of the customer."

> DOROTHY CRANFORD, Real Estate Officer
> First Madison Valley Bank
> Ennis, Montana

"We feel uncomfortable asking for business. There is an unwritten rule that customers should want to come up to us and that asking for their business is *not* professional."

> BRENDA ALLRED, Operations Officer
> First National Bank of DAC
> Las Cruces, New Mexico

"Generally speaking, people who got into banking ten or more years ago did so because they liked order taking, not sales."

> DIANE McCARTNEY, Vice President
> Promenade National Bank
> Richardson, Texas

Think about the comments you've read and then answer the question for yourself, "Why is it difficult for bankers to be marketing-oriented?" Think about how we defined *marketing* in Chapter 1. We said that marketing is finding out what the customer wants and delivering the product or service at a price the customer will pay, at a place and in a manner the customer chooses. But in most of the answers we received, bankers confused "selling" with "marketing." Marketing is the overall process while selling, or "helping" as we call it, is the point after the customer's needs are identified that the product or service is offered and commitment from the customer is gained.

The "Nobody Told Me" Syndrome

One of the main themes our surveys revealed was "nobody told me" that banks should be marketing-oriented. Many comments included such phrases as "the customers have always come to us," "times have changed," "bankers are numbers-oriented," "bankers haven't been trained in marketing and sales." In effect, one big reason that bankers have not been marketing-oriented is that we didn't know we needed to be.

The "I Don't Have To Do It" Syndrome

Another major theme we heard from bankers was the idea that since customers come to the bank and since many of our services are unique, "I don't have to do it." These comments were given to us: "Banking is regulated," "We've had a monopoly," "We're too busy waiting on the customers and filling out reports." In Chapter 1, we mentioned four major beliefs historically held by bankers. The first was this: We have products and services that are "different" and scarce, and our role is to properly ration them.

These comments reflect past times. Today's bankers no longer believe this.

The "I Don't Want To Do It" Syndrome

Now we come to one of the major stumbling blocks. Do you remember the question that we asked at the beginning of this book? "How many of you *like* to sell?" We maintain that the major reason bankers are not marketing-oriented or sales-oriented is that they simply don't want to be. Ask yourself, "Do I like to sell?"—and see how you answer the question. We suspect that much more than 5 to 15 percent of those who read this book will say "yes," because those who hate selling won't even buy the book, much less read it.

WHY DON'T BANKERS LIKE TO SELL?

Our second major belief that we shared in Chapter 1 was this: Salespeople are unprofessional and pushy, as personified by the offensive used-car salesman; therefore, selling is something we consciously and subconsciously do not want to do.

In our seminars and training programs for banks, savings and loans, credit unions and their trade associations, the above belief is still prevalent in most audience members. Is *selling* really as bad as that? Yes—and no. Yes, there are still pushy salespeople in many industries, including the automobile business. But even that is changing, as can be seen in the examples that follow.

Sewell Village Cadillac

Carl Sewell is the second generation owner of one of the premier Cadillac dealerships in America. Buying a car from Sewell, and getting it serviced properly after the sale, is truly a unique experience. No hard sell, no pushy salespeople. Instead, you find professionally trained, experienced, well-dressed salespeople who want to meet customer needs. Chuck Bellows is your classic nice guy complete with a laid-back style and a country twang. He's been selling Cadillacs for 28 years. His goal is not just to make one sale but to get and keep the customer for life. The service personnel feel the same way.

Carl Sewell's book, *Customers For Life*, was published by Doubleday in October of 1990. If you think that car salespeople are bad role models, then read his book. It might give you a new perspective on selling.

Goodson Acura

We walked into an Irving, Texas, Nissan dealership in September of 1990. As we wandered through the showroom looking at 300Zs we noticed five salespeople, four male and one female, clustered near the center of the carpeted sales area. A couple looked up as we examined the cars. None of them came over.

Fifteen minutes later we walked out of the showroom. As we got into our Sewell Cadillac a young woman rushed outside and asked if anyone had helped us. We said "no." She apologized, said she was in public relations, had noticed we had been ignored and asked us to come back in so she could get someone to help us. We declined but made it clear that we were serious buyers. She apologized again and we drove off.

In fact, we drove into the Acura dealership next door. We had heard of the Acura quality and wanted to see it firsthand.

At Goodson Acura we were greeted by a receptionist who promptly found a salesman to talk with us as we looked at the cars on the floor. Ben Nabors is a clean-cut young man whose sales ability was fine, but more importantly it was his attitude and willingness to accommodate our needs that were outstanding.

Throughout the three or four days of the buying period, driving the car, looking at the trade-in, etc., the entire process was handled professionally. On Sunday, September 2, we decided to try to make a deal for the Legend that was sitting on the showroom floor. The negotiations, the financing, were all handled on the spot. And we took the car home with us an hour later. (As an aside, does this show how tough the competition for financing is? How many of you are open on Sundays and have competitive leasing programs?)

As the financing papers were being drawn, we were greeted by a woman who said she would be our service representative in the future. She carefully went over a three-page checklist designed to acquaint us with the car and the agency's service department.

Did we feel we had been treated well? You bet we did. Had we been sold? Yes, and we enjoyed every minute of it because they met our needs. The moral to these two stories is obvious: helping customers get what they want in a professional manner is the essence of selling, regardless of whether the product is cars or money. And one last comment: Goodson Acura personnel told us that they had recently been named Acura's number one dealer in service in the country. Their role model: Sewell Village Cadillac.

The "I Don't Know How To" Syndrome

One last reason why bankers are not market- or sales-oriented is a very legitimate one—many simply don't have the know-how. Surely top management can't expect employees to sell if they don't know how. And, really, that's the reason for this book: to show bankers how to sell.

SUMMARY

This chapter has been designed to remind the reader why bankers don't like to sell, and to explain how their inadequacies can be overcome. Our survey revealed deeply ingrained banker resistance to marketing and sales ideas. And yet, virtually every banker we've met agrees that competition, new products and services, the need for stronger relationships, and chaotic economic times force bankers to change. Those bankers who survive and thrive in the Nineties will embrace the concepts and strategies outlined in this book.

CHAPTER 3

The Source of New Bank Business: Qualifying Present Customers

Studies have shown that up to 60 percent of new business comes from present customers. Why do customers choose one bank over another, and how do we identify additional needs? These questions are the subject of this chapter.

FRIENDLY, EMPATHETIC EMPLOYEES— THEY LIKE YOU

Even with today's high-tech approach to financial services, customers still appreciate being helped by smiling tellers and customer service reps; customers even enjoy an empathetic approach from loan officers who sometimes must say "no." Ask yourself this question: When you buy groceries, get a haircut, eat at a restaurant or get your clothes dry-cleaned, do you find someone you don't like to do business with? Or, like most individuals, do you find yourself trading with people you like?

Have you ever walked into a bank where no one was smiling, the lobby felt like a morgue, the tellers had their heads down and the atmosphere was downright cold? How did it feel?

Now think about the lobby brimming with activity, friendly yet businesslike conversation, helpful people with smiling faces who treat you like you're the special person you are. Does it matter to a customer? You bet!

■ ■ ■

Always remember, customers buy from people they like.

■ ■ ■

SAFETY AND CONVENIENCE— THEY TRUST YOU

Customers bank with you because they are afraid to keep their cash at home under the mattress. They want valuables kept safely and they want access to their funds through check writing, credit card and other transferring methods. Customers want a convenient location, ATMs, longer customer hours, a pleasant physical facility, comfortable chairs, short teller lines, etc.

KNOWLEDGE

The third attraction that makes customers choose one bank over another is knowledge. It's not enough that our staff is friendly and likeable. It's not enough that customers trust us. They also expect us to know what we're doing. We believe a customer has the right to expect at least the following from bank employees:

- That a Customer Service Representative (CSR) understands every detail of the various types of deposit accounts the bank offers. In the book *Service Quality,* a test on financial products knowledge was given to CSRs and customers. CSRs scored 44 percent and customers scored 36 percent. In other words, CSRs' knowledge of the bank's products exceeded those of the customer by only 8 percent, not nearly enough for a business where information is one of the major "products" being sold. A bank employee's lack of knowledge can prove costly to a customer.

- That a teller can count money accurately (is this tough?), understands when availability of funds will occur, has enough business law and negotiable instrument knowledge to function properly, is office-machine literate and has common sense enough to know that smoking and chewing gum are not acceptable on the job.
- That a loan secretary can use word processing, knows documentation requirements, can handle most of the loan officer's business in his or her absence and has a cursory understanding of financial statements.

We could continue but we think you get our drift: bankers are perceived as financial experts—knowledge of our business, knowledge of the community and the economy, and knowledge of customer needs is essential. Customers expect that bank employees have received significant training, an assumption that in some banks is far from accurate.

An important side benefit: *knowledge* instills confidence. Customers want to work with bank employees who are confident and know what they are doing. A lack of job-related skills and product knowledge affects self-confidence and undermines a person's self-esteem. It is more difficult to help a customer if basic financial knowledge is missing.

COMMUNICATION

The fourth element that can successfully differentiate one bank from its competitors is the ability of its employees to communicate. It's not enough to smile and be friendly, to be trustworthy and to possess a vast store of knowledge if none of these qualities is communicated. In fact, many of a bank's competitors, such as brokerage houses, are so good at communication that a customer may buy elsewhere simply because of television and other advertising that attracts the customer with such phrases as the following:

"We have the edge you need to meet any financial challenge."

THE PRINCIPAL FINANCIAL GROUP

"To find a more popular way to fight taxes than our investment, you have to go back a long way."

MERRILL LYNCH

"Peace of mind. When you work hard all day, you shouldn't have to lose sleep worrying about your investments."

KEMPER FINANCIAL

Fortunately, advertising is only a small part of communication. More important is the ability of an individual in a bank to communicate orally, either in person or by phone, and in writing, to existing or prospective customers. Since most selling opportunities are handled in person or by phone, let's look at a few of the essential communication skills that bankers should possess:

- Good telephone skills
- Courtesy
- A reasonable command of the English language, and in some markets, Spanish or Asian language skills are also necessary
- Empathy
- The ability to pose questions without conducting an interrogation
- The ability to listen

Many bankers possess an abundance of skills in some or all of these areas. But here's the key—is a banker born with these skills? We think not. They are learned. And they must be taught. How much time and money do banks spend on "soft" skills like these? Not enough, we suspect.

Let's consider now how the combination of *like, trust, knowledge* and *communication* come together in "helping" an existing customer purchase additional bank products or services. When this process succeeds it is known to all of us in this industry by the buzzword *cross-selling*.

IDENTIFYING NEEDS

There are essentially five elements in the sales process: prospecting, identifying needs, presenting, handling objections and gaining commitment. Many great sales trainers use three or four or six. Prospecting is step one but is sometimes unnecessary when dealing with present customers. So our book begins with identifying needs and we save prospecting for Chapter 7. Let's first examine how to sell present customers while they are in the bank.

WHAT ARE WE TRYING TO ACCOMPLISH?

The concept of selling as we define it encompasses what is known as "consultative" or "relationship" selling. This consultative selling process is very different from the traditional sales methods that bankers abhor. Think of the process as one of "need fulfillment."

The traditional way of selling reminiscent of the pushy salesperson saw the selling process from a time-and-emphasis approach as a pyramid, like that in Figure 3.1.

The biggest portion of the time with the customer was spent in persuading the customer to buy your product even if it was not in the customer's best interest, deftly handling all possible objections with smooth rhetoric. Many customers were turned off and simply did not buy. Others bought but later resented having been pushed into buying. So even the gratification that came with need satisfaction was dampened by the approach of the salesperson.

Contrast the foregoing example with the consultative, helping approach as illustrated in Figure 3.2.

Notice in Figure 3.2 that the time and emphasis are placed on *identifying the customer's needs and wants*. This approach

FIGURE 3.1   Traditional Selling

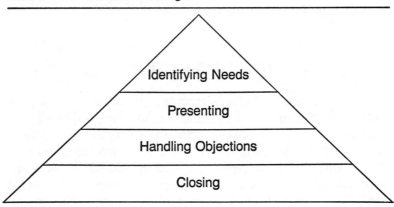

is one that is totally consistent with what bankers already want to do—help the customer. Doesn't it stand to reason that the first thing a banker should do in an attempt to be of service is to identify customer needs? In other words, the approach that we're suggesting centers on the customer's needs. If there is no need, then why try to sell something? Have you ever had someone try to sell you something you didn't need? Was your reaction one of resistance? Well, bank customers may feel the same

FIGURE 3.2   Consultative, Helpful Selling

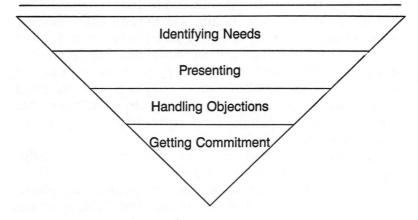

way. Similarly, bank employees will resist selling anything this way because most bank employees don't like to sell anyway.

HOW TO ASSESS EXISTING CUSTOMER NEEDS

The qualifying process has three distinct phases. They may take some time with new or unknown customers, but are quickly consolidated with the existing customers we are addressing in this section. The phases are:

1. Building rapport
2. Asking qualifying questions
3. Listening and summarizing understanding

Rapport Building

Earlier in this chapter we discussed the idea that most people consider whether they like a bank's personnel as an important factor in their willingness to buy. Since we are considering in this chapter the idea of getting to "yes" with an existing customer, we can make an assumption that the customer already has a good feeling toward the bank's employees. In many cases you, personally, know the customer and building rapport may not be necessary since it already exists. But one word of caution: If there is any doubt about whether your customer is comfortable with you, spend extra time here. It will help immensely in the overall selling process.

Now, how do you go about establishing rapport? Well, that depends. First, let's understand exactly what we mean by rapport. Rapport is a feeling of trust between individuals wherein a customer can feel comfortable in providing you with confidential information about such intimate matters as money. In many cases you begin to establish rapport when you engage in "small talk." Ask yourself how many times, whether you are a CEO or a CSR, you begin a customer conversation with one of these phrases:

- How's it going?
- Is it hot (cold, wet) out there today?
- Have you had enough/too much rain?
- How's business?
- How is your family?
- How are you feeling?

All of these phrases are just ways to open a conversation and begin establishing rapport. Notice that we normally ask questions so that the customer will talk. In many cases we're genuinely concerned about a customer's health or business. In others, it is merely an icebreaker. Under either circumstance it often smoothes the way for the process of determining the customer's needs.

Asking Questions

Whether the question is, How are you? or Why do you think our bookkeeping department is rude?, the manner in which you ask the question is crucial. A sincere desire to help the customer should be obvious in the tone of voice. And don't forget to call the customer by name often.

Discovering customer needs calls for open-ended questions at first. They give the customer a chance to talk and tell you about the things they need or want. Open-ended questions? Start with who, when, where, what, how, why, and tell me. Here are some typical open-ended questions:

- Tell me what you need in a checking account.
- What are your plans for retirement?
- When do you think you might need the money?
- How would you like to open this account?
- How will this loan be of benefit to you?
- What specific products and services do you look for in a bank?

Then listen. Really tune in to what the customer is saying. In most cases the customer's response will lead to follow-up questions such as these:

- Are you saying that your preference in checking accounts is one in which you can write as many checks as possible and avoid any service charges?
- If I understand you correctly, you don't have any specific need to access the money at present, but you would prefer a 90-day maximum period to be assured of getting the money without paying a penalty. Is that correct?
- You've indicated that the loan would enable you to expand into other states. Are there enough qualified managers in the organization to handle the expansion or will you be needing help from other sources?
- You've indicated a need for a variety of products and services. Which ones may we help you with first?

Remember: The objective is to fully determine customer needs before attempting to fulfill them. The conversation should flow smoothly, but be careful about asking sensitive questions. We recommend asking permission to ask sensitive questions. For instance,

"Do you mind if I ask why you might not want to tie your money up a bit longer to get our highest rate?"

In the initial phase of need identification, we ask open-ended questions designed to draw the customer out. To get points clarified or move the discussion to a decision, use closed probes.

Closed probes are helpful when your goal is to get a specific answer—often a yes or no. Think of questions like these once you have moved past your initial open-ended questions:

- "Then your preference for our flexible interest rate CD is a term of two years, is that correct?"
- "Do I understand that you want a car loan where you have to put as little down as possible?"
- "Is your major concern that you be able to access the balance quickly?"

When you're dealing with an existing customer, this type of questioning should be fairly easy. You already have access to personal information, and they, in turn, already know something about the bank. Developmental probes are designed merely to allow customers to expand or elaborate on their needs. Closed probes give you *specific* information about an aspect of the customer's need. When you have fully identified the need, then it is time for the summary probe.

Listening and Summarizing Understanding

Obviously, you are listening throughout the qualifying process. The test of your effectiveness at listening and communicating is in how well you now understand the customer's need. To assure yourself and the customer that there is no misunderstanding, ask summary questions such as these:

- "If my notes are right then, you'll want a checking account with overdraft protection, a one-year certificate of deposit for $30,000, a safety deposit box and you want to meet a consumer loan officer who can give you facts on our automobile financing. Is that correct?"
- "So you'll need two cashiers checks, one for $1,500 to the State of Alabama and the other for $450 to the County Tax-Assessor?"
- "As I understand it, you're interested in a way of moving money from one account to another without having to write checks or come to the bank, is that right?"

Once the need has been identified, only then should the product or service be presented that will meet the need. Remember: You can't give customers what they want until you discover what is wanted. Also, in many cases what the customer wants is a benefit, e.g., to receive service, to make money, to save money. Your job is to meet the customer's expectations with products or services that produce those benefits.

HOW THEY DID IT

Many bankers want tellers to cross-sell. This is difficult when speed and accuracy in the teller transaction are of utmost importance. Asking questions can pay off, though, as John F. Varner III found out. He is now a management trainee at First Commerce Bank in Commerce, Georgia. Here is his story: "Working as a teller I was able to land a large loan for the bank that would not have been made any other way. I was helping a new customer and found he was developing a large parcel of land as an industrial park. I told him about our president who was the same age as the young developer. I set up a meeting for the two, and as a result, the developer started using the bank's loan services in addition to the personal checking account."

BancFirst is a $700 million Oklahoma bank holding company with 14 offices across the state. One of their senior executives, Ralph McCalmont, had the vision to institute a training program for CSRs and others throughout the organization. We were involved in that effort.

Here's how the CSRs work. First, they have access to significant information on present customer activity. Having this knowledge on hand gives the CSR confidence to ask questions about other needs. On a daily basis the CSR can qualify for incentive pay simply by asking questions and offering services even if the customer fails to buy. A copy of their report form is shown in Figure 3.3.

Here's an example of how attention to the sales process paid off. Laurie, in Stillwater, Oklahoma, asked an elderly customer why such a large amount of money wasn't earning interest but rather was in a demand deposit account. The customer responded that she needed constant access due to illness. Follow-up questions resulted in the customer's moving $10,000 from a competitor; dates on maturing CDs were determined for future action.

(Some bankers would cringe at the idea of disturbing the large demand deposit account to begin with. The lesson learned here is that relationships count. Do what's in the customer's best interest and it will pay off.)

FIGURE 3.3 CSR Reporting Form

Initial Request　　= I
Offer　　　　　　= O
Referral　　　　　= R
Successful Cross-Sell = X

Week Beginning _____
CSR Name _____
Location _____

Date	Customer (N = New)	Ckg	D.D.	ATM	C.C.	MC/V	Sav	CD	Trust	SD Box	Tr Ck	IRA	Lnd	ACH	Misc	Referred To	Comments

Total (T) _____
Total (O) _____
Total (R) _____
Total (X) _____

Source: Developed by McCuistion and Associates with BancFirst.

Consultative selling means satisfying needs and solving problems. It takes into consideration that discovering what the customer wants and needs, then meeting that need, is the essence of the sales/helping process. It is not pushing on a customer what you have, but adapting to what is in the best possible interest of that customer, that earns you a customer for life.

SUMMARY

The first step in helping (or cross-selling) an existing customer is identifying needs. Most of the sales process occurs here. The banker's role is that of a consultant who, by asking pertinent questions, discovers what the customer wants. It is here that rapport is so important. Customers value generic benefits in a banking relationship. They want to deal with a bank they trust, with employees they like and with staff who are knowledgeable and with whom they can communicate. The banker's first goal is to establish rapport and listen carefully to what the customer wants.

CHAPTER 4

Presenting the Right Product to the Right Customer at the Right Time

In the previous chapter on qualifying, we emphasized the importance of building rapport and identifying customer needs. The better the job is done in the initial "helping" phase, the easier is the entire process. In fact, so important are building rapport and assessing customer needs that both must be present throughout the entire process. In this chapter we will discuss the second phase of the selling process, that of *presenting* the product or service that best meets the customer's needs. *How* and *when* the product or service is presented becomes just as crucial as the product or service itself. Throughout this chapter, as is done throughout the entire book, our emphasis will be on providing benefits to the customer that meet the customer's needs.

HOW NOT TO DO IT

Here are a few examples that we've observed in dealing with bankers. Most have to do with customer service/new account representatives or loan officers.

The "Here's the Brochure, You Decide" Technique

A potential customer walks up to a new accounts desk and is invited to sit down.

Customer: I'd like to open a checking account."

New Accounts: "Great. We've got six accounts to choose from, one with no minimum balance but lots of service charges, one that requires $1,000 minimum balance but lets you write lots of checks, one with a $2,000 minimum balance with the ability to write six checks a month and we'll pay you interest at $5\frac{1}{4}$ percent, one that..."

How is a confused customer supposed to respond? The new-accounts representative has totally skipped the identifying needs step. An account may be opened, but will a relationship be created? We doubt it. And is the customer being steered into the right checking account?

Credit Life: Should a Customer Buy It?

Loan officers have excellent opportunities to sell credit life insurance. And they have a great advantage of already having significant customer information on file. Is this what happens in your bank?

Loan Officer: "I assumed that you wouldn't want credit life or accident and health insurance so just initial in the indicated places."

Strong sales approach, huh? Or try this one:

Loan Officer: "We can provide credit life and disability coverage on this loan for just a few dollars a month."

Customer: Well, I don't know, I've got a life insurance policy through my company already."

Loan Officer: "All right, no problem."

In today's employee benefit environment, most customers have very little in the way of group life insurance. Besides, the loan officer never even probed for the customer's need or for the amount of present insurance, both of which would have been valuable information for the file even if the customer still failed to buy. In our opinion, the vast majority of today's consumer loan customers are underinsured and the loan officer has a responsibility, not only to the bank but to the customer, to provide every opportunity for a customer to protect his or her family from a financial problem that would result from an untimely death or illness.

THE NEED FOR PRODUCT KNOWLEDGE

Before getting to the actual presenting phase itself, we should strongly emphasize the need for employees to thoroughly understand the bank's products and services, as we mentioned earlier.

In other words customers have the right to expect that we are the experts in our own products and services. Remember that knowledge is one of the four key qualities that influence customers to choose our bank over a competitor.

One of our clients, BancFirst in Oklahoma, provides a minimum nine hours of intensive product knowledge training for its CSRs each year, and that's in addition to extensive training when they are initially hired. It's also in addition to sales and customer service training in the entire sales process.

Here are two other important reasons for extensive product knowledge:

1. An employee needs confidence in order to help a customer. One of the biggest confidence builders is knowledge. The old saying that knowledge is power is true. If you are sure of yourself, feel that you can answer virtually any question and understand how a specific product or service can benefit the customer, you will be much more effective.
2. How can employees cross-sell products they don't understand? Frankly, our research indicates that this is a major reason why some employees just will not cross-sell even if they have more than average sales ability.

Consider these problems, on top of the inherent problem that most bankers don't like to sell anyway, and you can understand the importance of training in product knowledge. Ironically, product knowledge is still lacking even though more training is provided in product knowledge than in selling skills. What does that tell you about the lack of sales training? Here's an eye-opening example of the importance of product knowledge.

When Ignorance Meets Incompetence

Longtime Texas banker Elmer B. Jenkins Jr. told us the story of one of his customer's experience in August of 1990. Elmer had just been named to head Comerica's branch office in the northern Dallas suburb of Richardson. One of his customers had a jumbo CD maturing and inquired as to Comerica's rate for 12 months. When told it was 7.3 percent he produced a newspaper ad showing an 8.3 percent rate at a competing bank down the street. As he was elderly and dependent on the interest to live, the extra $1,000 was important. Elmer empathized and wished him well.

The next day the customer was back in the bank with his check in hand. Elmer asked him what had happened and the customer related an incredible story.

Seems he had walked into the other bank, asked for someone who handled CDs and was directed to a nice young person who offered to help. However, the CD employee was unaware of the offer, didn't know about the ad and referred him to an officer. The officer had no knowledge either. Finally, it became apparent that no one in the entire branch knew about it or could authorize the rate. The customer left bewildered.

Elmer Jenkins and Comerica had the customer back. The other bank? Your guess is as good as theirs.

THE PHILOSOPHY OF PRESENTING

Remember that presenting the product or service is the second in a series of four steps designed to get a present customer to "yes." Because the customer already banks with you, the process is easier. Assuming that the initial qualifying step has gone smoothly, presenting should be relatively simple.

But keep in mind two overriding objectives of presenting:

1. Gaining or solidifying a relationship by satisfying the customer
2. Making the sale

To the extent that you have created the appropriate environment, the presentation will be easier. Consider your physical environment for a moment. Do you work in a private office? Can phone calls and interruptions be eliminated? If not, why not? What kind of relationship can be built with constant interruptions? Can the conversation be overhead by others waiting to be helped? Can the transaction be handled in a manner that acknowledges the importance of the customer's time?

Finally, we encourage you to see presenting for what it is—a part of the process of getting to "yes." Presenting *prior* to understanding needs will inevitably lead to many objections and make gaining commitment difficult.

THE PRESENTATION ITSELF

Remember that helping is a process. In most cases you won't actually think that step one, qualifying, is over and it's time to move into presenting. The process should flow. Try these three steps in the presentation stage.

Step 1: Clarify the need.   Bank employees should have taken careful notes in the qualifying phase. The first part of presenting is to repeat to the customer your understanding of the need.

Here are a few examples:

*   "I understand that you write about 30 checks per month and keep an average balance of about $1,000. Is that correct?"

- "My understanding is that you could bring another $20,000 to our bank if we could offer another quarter percent on the published rate. Is that right?"
- "As I understand it, you will be retiring at age 65, or five years from now, so the major benefits you want are tax deferral and a high rate of return, is that accurate?"
- "You've expressed a desire for a checkbook system that has two copies plus an original. Is that correct?"
- "You presently have two checking accounts here plus a savings account and you want to be sure that no checks are ever returned should an error be made. Is that your major concern?"
- "At your previous bank you really enjoyed the convenience of automatic payroll deposit, credit card overdraft protection and a free safe deposit box based on their club account. Is that right?"

In other words, check to be sure that your understanding meets that customer's needs. Get affirmative feedback at this point *prior* to proceeding to the next step.

Step 2: Mention product or service and determine customer familiarity.   Do not assume that your customer understands the product or service. Always begin with and emphasize the benefits to the customer. Keep uppermost in your mind the WIIFM philosophy: the customer always wants to know "what's in it for me." Here are some examples:

- "Our check-it-out account will enable you to write an unlimited number of checks with no service charge to you. The only requirement is that you maintain a minimum balance of $1,000 at all times. You've indicated a desire for a flexible, low-cost account. Would this meet your needs?"
- "Because you are able to bring an additional $20,000 to our bank, may I suggest that you invest your funds in our Super Duper Maxi CD which pays one-quarter percent over the normal rate. Additionally, we can guarantee this rate for six months."
- "Mrs. Brown, your needs for a good return and tax deferral can best be met by purchasing an annuity that will pay you

over $1,000 a month for 25 years after your retirement.
Would the security of knowing that your funds are safe and
earning a fine return be of benefit to you?"

- "Mr. Black, you want at least two copies of your checks.
We can offer you a system that has two carbons for about
$250 per thousand or, if you prefer, a third carbon system
for only $25 more. Which would be your preference?"

- "Mrs. Smith, we can offer you a worry-free account that
has automatic overdraft protection. Since you travel a lot
and your commission checks arrive at different times of the
month, this protection will allow you to eliminate the embarrassment and cost of returned checks."

- "Jim, I know you want to re-establish your credit after
some tough economic times. May I suggest that you borrow
money against your savings and repay it over a 12-month
period? This way, your credit record will be enhanced and
you should soon be able to get additional credit in your
own name."

Be careful to mention benefits as well as features. A *feature*
is an item of information about a product or service. A *benefit*
is specifically what it will do for the customer. For instance:

The feature: "This money market account allows you
three withdrawals per quarter with no charge and pays
interest at 8 percent."

The benefit: "You are able to earn our highest rate offered on this type of account and still have immediate
access to your funds."

The feature: "This account comes with automatic overdraft protection."

The benefit: "You will never have to worry about the
embarrassment of a returned check. Plus you'll be able
to borrow money without even coming into the bank."

The feature: "Your employer can deposit your pay-
check directly into your account."

The benefit: "Your check will automatically be deposited, thereby saving you time, and your money will be credited faster as well."

The feature: "Our trust department will invest your funds safely, render an accounting on a monthly basis, credit the income to your checking account monthly, complete all necessary tax returns, and counsel with you at your convenience."

The benefit: "Your funds will be safe and your income will be at your disposal automatically. There's no need to worry about tax returns and accounting, as we will handle all these things."

Step 3: Enhance the relationships. Normally referred to as "cross-selling," a term with negative connotations, the presenting phase gives ample opportunities for expanding the relationship. Every banker should constantly be aware of how to meet additional customer needs as they become known. Here are some examples:

- "Now, Mrs. Lunday, would you prefer that we give you a receipt and hold your certificate of deposit in safekeeping or would you like to take it with you?"
"I'll take it if I may."
"Of course. Now do you need a safe deposit box to hold your CD and your other valuable papers?"
- "Mr. Battle, while the note is being prepared, could we discuss other ways in which we might be of service? I see that you have teenage children. Our bank prides itself on helping our customers with education loans, and special college checking accounts. And when it comes time for them to establish credit, we'd like to offer our services and work with them."
- "I'm almost through completing your checking account papers and your overdraft protection application. By the way, have you considered opening a savings account? Our club account enables you to have all these services plus free travelers checks, ATM cards for you and your spouse, and a dis-

counted price on a safe deposit box, all for only seven dollars a month."

Many times these offers to help with other bank services uncover additional needs that may have been missed in the qualifying phase. Always be alert to ways to enhance the relationships.

Two caveats: Never push. Be efficient in using the customer's time. Different people react differently. If you sense that a customer wants to just "get on with it," then just get on with it. It never hurts to inquire as to how much time they have. Obviously, your time is valuable, too.

SUMMARY

Presenting is the second phase of the helping process. To the extent that you have qualified well, the presenting will be a relatively easy consequence of need fulfillment. Remember that the customer is interested in benefits, not features. Customers generally want to buy, not be sold. So don't be pushy.

Up to this point you have asked, questioned, listened, probed and asked for feedback, made recommendations and outlined benefits. Throughout the process you have encouraged questions and tried to enhance the relationship. No doubt every customer will buy immediately and willingly, right? Not necessarily. Read on to see how we can handle objections.

CHAPTER 5

Handling Objections: Turning "No" or "Maybe" into "Yes"

We truly believe that a great advantage of consultative selling, of helping customers fulfill their needs, is that it eliminates or severely limits the customer's objections to buying from our bank. After all, if we correctly assess the customer's needs by asking the right questions, we create an environment of true rapport. If we present appropriate solutions to these needs, then how can a customer not be sold?

The reality is that, no matter how good a job we do, there will still be customer resistance. When objections do occur, it usually signals a need for more information. Let's examine what objections are, why they occur and, most importantly, how to handle them and get the transaction back on the track to commitment.

WHY DO CUSTOMERS OBJECT?

An objection is any reason that prevents the customer from buying. It is a reason, an argument, a question that hinders the customer from committing to the bank's product or service. We will discuss four primary causes for customers' objections. If you understand why customers object, you pave the way for eliminating the objections and can actually enhance customer commitment. Let's examine the major obstacles.

Cause 1: Fear

Customers are oftentimes afraid; their fears are valid for them. A customer may be afraid to make the wrong decision. The customer may be afraid to tie up money for too long or too short a time. The customer may be afraid to accept the interest rate offered or may want to negotiate or trade elsewhere. The customer may fear making a choice: choose an account with a high versus a low minimum balance, put money that might be needed soon into an IRA or choose cash management options that might lessen control over their funds.

Many times fear is a consequence of the customer's lack of knowledge. If you can provide sufficient information and if the customer trusts you, often this obstacle can be overcome.

Cause 2: Lack of Communication

Often the customer simply hasn't understood your presentation and how the offered product or service meets the required needs. Ask probing questions to build a bridge to better communication.

Cause 3: The Nagging Negotiator

Some customers will object to virtually anything offered—you know the type. They always want just one-quarter more in the rate on CDs or else want to pay just one-quarter less. They ask for free checks with another service or no service charges or promise great things in a future relationship. To these people, the "sale" is a game. They want the best terms available and will haggle because they enjoy haggling.

Cause 4: The Valid Objection

As we mentioned before, all objections are valid if they prevent the consummation of the transaction. The most valid objection a customer can make, in our estimation, is by correctly pointing out that the product or service presented will be clearly inadequate to meet his or her needs. This can be embarrassing and is usually attributed to the banker's failure to complete the qualifying phase successfully. Making a successful sale under this circumstance may well hinge upon whether or not the customer will be patient, as the banker, in effect, starts the process over again.

Another valid objection occurs when the customer lacks the authority to make a decision. Good qualifying early on should ascertain this possibility and allow for it in the selling process.

OVERCOMING OBJECTIONS

We will discuss some critical factors in successfully overcoming objections. How these are dealt with separates the novice from the professional helper.

Watch Your Attitude

The way that an objection is handled is crucial. This is no time for defensiveness, confrontation, frustration or ignoring the objection. Tempting as it may be, taking a condescending approach toward the customer is a sure way to lose not only the present transaction, but perhaps the entire relationship.

Listen with Empathy

The key to overcoming objections is to understand the problem. It has been said that since each of us has two ears and one mouth perhaps we should use them in that proportion. This is the time to really listen. Sometimes it requires listening "between the lines"; i.e., the customer may say one thing and mean another. For example, "I have adequate insurance coverage" may mean "your insurance premiums are too high."

The listening process should always be done with empathy but it is especially important now. Put yourself in the customers' position; see the objection from *their* point of view. This doesn't mean you will necessarily agree, much less give in. It simply means you are actively listening. If fear or communication is the problem, then the sooner you understand it, the sooner the objection can be overcome. Active listening sets the stage for the next phase—that of asking probing questions to re-ascertain customers' needs.

Ask Probing Questions

Once you've heard the customer's objections, a good technique is to merely relate your understanding back to the customer along with a question that solicits customer feedback. Here are examples:

- "As I understand it, your concern is that you might need the money *prior* to retirement. Is that correct?"
- "Are you saying that you could move another $20,000 to our bank if we could meet the other bank's rate on one-year certificates?"
- "Mr. Johnson, you seem to be saying that you're concerned with the soundness of our bank. Is that your main objection to what I've previously outlined?"

Other questions that may be especially useful in handling objections include:

- "What precisely would you have to have in a line of credit to move your banking business to our bank?"
- "Is there any other information about our trust department's performance that I could provide for you?"

The overall objective in asking these and other questions is to clarify, to narrow and define the objection so it can be dealt with. The attitude and spirit of these questions is exemplified by these examples:

- "I can appreciate your concern." [Agreement and empathy] "Help me to understand what is most important to you. What, specifically, would you like your savings to do for you?" [Questions to clarify]
- "Is there something I've not fully explained?"
- "It appears to me that you may still be concerned about. . ."
- "How will you be arriving at your decision?"
- "What else do you need from me to make a decision?"

PROVIDE INFORMATION: ANSWER THE OBJECTIONS

Once you have a firm understanding of what stands in the way of gaining customer commitment, you have two major choices:

1. Agree that the customer's objections are valid and that the bank simply cannot meet them. For example, a customer who insists on a significantly higher rate on a certificate of deposit than your bank is willing to pay may leave you with no option but to offer best wishes. Remember the Comerica example in Chapter 4 wherein the money was returned to Elmer Jenkins the next day when a competitor failed to help the customer? That Comerica's Jenkins handled the customer well when losing a CD over interest rate paved the way for a return of the business.

2. Answer the objection by providing information that overcomes the objection. This choice is obviously preferable and can rescue what might otherwise have been a lost sale. Your customer wants benefits. Additional information or clarifying/reiterating previous information may be all it takes. Be honest, be factual. The customer needs to know that he or she is getting a good deal. Re-emphasize the benefits and help the customer to appreciate the value in the transaction. Remember that the objective here is to maintain and enhance a present customer relationship. Your ability to impress the customer with your knowledge of his or her needs as well as your knowledge of the bank's products and services will go a long way toward gaining commitment.

ASK FOR ACCEPTANCE

After you've answered the objection to the best of your ability, the next step is to ask if the information you've given satisfies the customer's concerns. You want feedback in order to move toward agreement or to find a need for further clarification. It is essential that the customer feel comfortable. If there is still confusion, do not go forward. Handle it!

Questions that ask for acceptance might include:

- "Will that solve the problem?"
- "Does this sound reasonable?"
- "Do you see this helping you?"
- "Is there any other information that I can provide you?"

Keep in mind that for the bank to win, the customer must win also. Handling objections is an art but one that can be acquired with practice and true customer orientation.

Ron Willingham, in his book and materials, *The Best Seller*, uses an approach with objections that is easy to remember and very effective. He calls it the "feel, felt, found approach." When a customer voices an objection, the banker can respond in the following way: "Mr. Long, I can appreciate how you feel. Others have felt the same way too. But often they have found that..."

This approach works so well because it acknowledges how the customer feels, thereby showing listening skills combined with empathy. It acknowledges that others have shared the customer's concerns. Finally, it handles the objection by pointing out positive experiences of others who have had the same objection.

SUMMARY

Here is a list of do's and don'ts in handling objections.

Do's:
- Be sensitive and empathetic.
- Find out what or who the customer is comparing you with.
- Use empathetic phrases:
  - I appreciate...
  - I respect...
  - I agree...
- Probe to gain understanding of the objection.
- Emphasize benefits to the customer.

- See price as only a part of the process. Discuss it, but only at the appropriate time and after you've shared value and benefits in excess of the price.

Don'ts:
- Be defensive or argumentative.
- Be pushy.
- Answer objections to price with: "It's out of my hands." "No, it isn't. Everyone else is charging the same." "Take it or leave it."
- Bluff. If you don't know an answer, admit it—then find out the answer.
- Make a commitment if you don't have the authority.

Though most customers will raise few objections, there is a positive angle. Welcome them as an opportunity to get closer to agreement! In some cases you will be well served to raise questions that customers normally ask. Then answer them. Always solicit customer feedback and input. One last positive thought on objections: they are the last step before gaining customer commitment. Read on.

CHAPTER 6

Gaining Commitment

In this chapter, we will discuss the final step in the sales and helping process: getting the customer's commitment. In consultative, relationship-building selling, asking for a commitment is actually the smallest part of the sales process and should be the easiest.

The major part of the sales process should be spent on step one—developing rapport and qualifying. Based on needs identified in step one, you offered the customer the products or services to help meet those needs, in step two, the presentation. You handled objections along the way or as outlined in the previous chapter, as step three. Asking for and getting a commitment is the fourth and final step.

"CLOSING" VERSUS "COMMITMENT"

One reason that most bankers hate selling and equate it with the pushy, used-car sales tactics is because most salespeople of 15 to 20 years ago were taught that the close was the key to making the sale. As a result, salespeople pushed their products or services on customers, spent most of the time struggling to overcome objections and used many techniques to close the sale. And in many cases, this style worked. Lots of sales were made. But few relationships were developed.

Since banking historically has been a relationship business and since our product, money, historically was scarce, pushing products on a customer was not only uncomfortable, it was unnecessary. It was and is downright undignified. So, over the years bankers developed the mind-set we mentioned in Chapter 1.

But, as always, circumstances change. Lots of companies are throwing money and financial services at bank customers. Competition, inflation, deregulation, all have eroded banking's market share. So now we all must be in the selling business. But it doesn't follow that we all must be pushy.

Because we are interested in a long term relationship and we have our customer's needs in mind, we sell (help) the customer products they need. The process is designed to gain their commitment to a product or service that fulfills their needs, not our sales quota. Now if both can happen simultaneously, all the better. But, above all, we want their commitment to a continued relationship, not a one-shot sale.

WHEN DO YOU ASK YOUR CUSTOMER
FOR COMMITMENT?

Selling is challenging and exciting because no two situations are alike and no two customers are alike. Thus, in one situation, the selling process could take an hour. In another, it's over in five minutes. Some customers know exactly what they want, communicate it clearly, require no "coddling," and just want fast service and no nonsense. Others must be led and spoon-fed, and require patience above all else.

Knowing customer buying styles can be very important. Even though a complete discussion of buying styles is outside the scope of this book, there are a few simple clues in body language which, if observed, can provide you with an idea of how the sale is proceeding and whether it is an opportune time to close. Figure 6.1 illustrates examples of positive and negative clues to body language.

Obviously, these clues are not foolproof but they can be indicators of a customer's intentions. The alert banker can adjust the sales approach to ensure more satisfactory results. Test neg-

FIGURE 6.1 Clues to Body Language

POSITIVE CLUES	NEGATIVE CLUES
Open arms — receptive	Tightly crossed arms — defensive, rejecting, closed
Leaning forward — receptive	Looking or leaning away — not ready, lost interest
Eye contact — interested	Rubbing nose — means "no"
Crossing legs toward you — interested and positive	Fingers forming a steeple — "I know this already"
Smiling, nodding head — receptive	Pushing chair away — negative and backing off
Questions, taking notes, objecting — interested	Crossing legs away — need to change your approach
	Doodling — redirect your focus, not interested
	Removing glasses — disagrees with you

ative gestures by asking a question which restates a customer's possible concern:

- "Do I have a proper understanding of your needs?"
- "You did indicate your desire for the highest rate, did you not?"

If the body language is negative, go slowly, refocus and re-confirm your understanding of the customer's needs.

Positive signs reinforce the fact that you are on the right track. Keep moving; get the commitment to flow naturally.

POSITIVE AND NEGATIVE FEEDBACK

During the sales process, the customer may signal a level of acceptance by asking questions that indicate a positive stance. These might include:

- "Is there a charge for an ATM card?"
- "How soon could I have approval?"
- "When can the paperwork be ready?"

The customer can also give us negative signs by making statements such as these:

- "I'm not sure that will work."
- "It's more money than I pay now."
- "The paperwork process takes too long."
- "Perhaps I'll come back later in the month."

Statements such as these should cause you to redirect and refocus the conversation. Something has been missed—inadequate qualifying, incomplete presentation or failure to develop rapport. Perhaps you failed to get adequate feedback throughout the process and did not deal adequately with objections along the way.

HOW TO ASK FOR COMMITMENT

The process of gaining commitment should permeate the entire sales process. Each time you present an appropriate point solicit customer feedback. This enables you to answer questions and deal with objections as you go through the process. It will also eliminate the element of surprise when a customer says no after sitting passively through a lengthy presentation. Remember—we want to *confirm* decisions all along the way.

Over the decades much study has been given to mistakes that salespeople make. One of the most frequent is simply not asking for the business. That's right—either overlooking the need to ask for commitment or else being reluctant to do so. Let's look at overlooking the need to ask.

Our experience is that the most common reason for not asking (other than reluctance) is simply that an employee is not trained to do so. No one ever taught bank employees how to sell and since salary wasn't tied to measurable results, it is easy to see how they overlooked asking for the business. But even if they understand the concept of asking, many employees simply don't know how to do it. One of our suggested techniques is to ask one or more "trial close" questions such as these:

- "How does that sound?"
- "How should we proceed?"
- "Is this loan term likely to meet your needs?"
- "What's our next step?"
- "Shall we go ahead and get the paperwork started?"

A customer's response to these questions will be an indicator of whether there are still objections to be handled or a misunderstanding to be cleared up or whether the customer is ready to buy. Tune in to body language clues. Do not be pushy, but do move the process toward a decision.

WHAT ABOUT RELUCTANCE TO ASK?

We believe that the most common reason why commitment isn't requested is that a salesperson is afraid of rejection. Ask yourself if you like rejection. No one does. So how do you avoid rejection? Simple. Don't ask for the sale, then you can't be told no. Unfortunately, neither can you help the customer, make money for the bank nor, ultimately, keep your job.

So how do we overcome reluctance to ask? Here are a couple of proven techniques.

- Consciously ask yourself this question: "What is the worst possible thing that could happen to me if I am told no? Now if you often answer, "The world would come to an end" or "I will die," then you may have a real problem. But we suspect that your answers would more closely resemble these: "I'll feel bad for a long time (about five minutes)." "My feelings will be hurt." "I'll miss my commission." "Nothing." "Oh, well, you win some, you lose some."

  It's natural to dislike rejection. But it is a fact of life that each of us has been and will be rejected many times in our lives. And we've lived to tell about, haven't we? So don't worry. Remember, it's how you react to rejection that is important because you have control over your reaction.

- Keep in mind the overall objective of building and enhancing relationships. What this means to you is that even though you will not make every sale, as long as you handle the selling process professionally, the relationship can be preserved and even enhanced.

WHAT IF THE PRODUCT OR SERVICE IS WRONG FOR THE CUSTOMER?

The acid test of a salesperson is to know how to handle a situation where the customer's needs are simply not best served by the bank's product or service. Suppose, for example, that your customer is totally dependent on interest income from investments to meet living expenses. Your bank's rates are clearly inferior to those of another investment source for a variety of reasons outside your control. Even though this customer likes and trusts you and your bank, you must graciously acknowledge that another source would be better, always keeping uppermost in your mind the customer's needs.

I many cases it may become obvious to you that the customer's needs are better served through other sources. Maintaining integrity in the sales process means that you should be the one to point this out to the customer. Doing so is not easy. What if you lose the entire relationship? It could happen. But, more likely, the customer will recognize your desire to serve his or her needs first. That recognition is a relationship builder, not a relationship destroyer.

The old style of selling was characterized by the salesperson's trying to force products and services on the customer regardless of the customer's needs. Bankers do, and should, reject that type of sales effort. Remember, we want to help our customers, not push products and services on them that they don't want.

GETTING TO "YES"

If we've handled the process correctly and can overcome our reluctance, then we get a "yes" by summarizing the transaction or benefits and simply asking for the business. Here are some examples.

- "Mrs. Customer, as you can see, our Command Cash Account will allow for automatic transfers to your checking account as needed. This will ensure that no checks will be returned should you be out of town or make a mistake. Shall I go ahead and type the cards for your signature?"
- "Mr. and Mrs. Moneybags, you can see the significant benefits of letting us do your financial plan. Your children will have a college fund set aside to ensure their education. Your insurance needs will be properly handled; you can be assured that funds will be available to cover living costs of the surviving spouse. And, perhaps best of all, your retirement funding will be in place, thus giving you peace of mind knowing that you have done the right thing. May I begin the initial step to get this process underway?"

CONFIRMING TECHNIQUES: ALTERNATE CHOICES

One of the simplest confirming techniques you can use is to present the customer with an alternative. Here are some examples.

- "Would you prefer the designer checks or the light blue?"
- "What is the better payment date, the first or the fifteenth?"
- "Would you prefer coming back to finalize this transaction on Monday or Tuesday?"
- "Can we put this money in a 90-day certificate or would six months be your preference?"

This type of "close" should be used only when you are comfortable that the customer is ready to commit. Old style salespeople manipulate the customer with this approach. They use this as a "nice" forced close. We never want to manipulate, but this is an excellent technique for gaining commitment.

BALANCE SHEET

The balance sheet technique is one that should be appropriate simply because of the business we're in. It is a method of comparing the pros and cons of two or more alternatives. It is designed to move the customer to an appropriate decision. Here are the advantages of each alternative.

Bank Advantages
- Cheaper Rate
- More flexible terms
- Personal service
- Can finance any model

Dealer Advantages
- More convenient
- Lower down payment

The idea is to weigh the advantages and disadvantages of each alternative and to prove (we hope) that bank financing represents a better deal. We recommend that you actually write the comparisons down in a "balance sheet" format. This makes comparison easy for your customer to understand.

Here's another piece of great news: When you are helping an existing customer, by definition you already have a relationship. To the extent that the relationship itself is strong, then one giant advantage to your getting the business is the relationship itself.

THE SALE BEGINS WITH "YES"

In relationship selling, the act of gaining commitment follows naturally the rapport building, qualifying step and the presentation. But once the customer agrees to the transaction, performance begins. It is essential that the employee be well versed in what he or she does and in how to consummate the transaction to the customer's satisfaction. Ineptness or significant time delays can disrupt the entire transaction, not to mention the relationship.

CHAPTER 7

Prospecting: How To Make the Outside Call

Thus far we believe that most of our readers are still fairly comfortable. Yes, we recognize that there is risk in the "helping" process. And, yes, we recognize the inherent aversion to change. Chapters 3 through 6 laid out a systematic approach to dealing with *existing* customers. We believe that most bankers welcome new ways to better serve customers and enhance present relationships. In this chapter, though, we're going to deliberately raise the frustration/anxiety level. Why? Because we're going to discuss the proactive step of calling on a customer or potential customer *outside* the bank. We'll focus mostly on developing new business, a process we refer to as prospecting.

WHY PROSPECT?

Did you ever want to return to those days of yesteryear when banks held a monopoly on most deposit and loan services, when all we had to do was wait for someone to come in and do business with us? That's not the way it is anymore. Many communities outside major metropolitan areas either are not growing or are actually losing population. And even if your bank is located in a growing area, inevitably some customers move, go out of business, change banks or die. In other words, to maintain bank profitability and to grow, it is necessary to constantly be acquiring new customers. And in case you've been under a rock for 20 years and haven't noticed, not every person and business in a bank's trade area automatically beats a path to the bank.

WHEN TO PROSPECT

Banks should prospect constantly. After all, we lose business constantly, don't we? Prospecting for new business is an essential part of virtually every business. Today, banks are no different.

Here are two questions for you:

1. Is your top management committed to actively seeking new business?
2. Do you, personally, like to solicit business outside the bank and, if so, is it easy to allocate the time to do so?

We would be surprised if many of you answered yes to both these questions—pleasantly surprised, but surprised nevertheless. Our experience with banks of all sizes, but particularly community banks, is that the business development or officer call program is at best a sporadic effort that is only marginally effective. Conversion to a sales culture requires a consistent program of constant prospecting.

WHAT IS PROSPECTING?

Prospecting is proactive: it is calling on an existing or potential customer outside the bank. Prospecting can be done by phone or in person. It may consist of several identifiable steps, which we'll cover in detail. In the classic sales process, this is the usual sequence of procedures:

1. Prospecting
2. Qualifying
3. Presenting
4. Handling objections
5. Gaining commitment

If this is the normal sequence of events, why have we saved the first step, prospecting, until last? There are two reasons.

1. Most of the time the customer is already in the bank so it is unnecessary.
2. Prospecting is the step most feared by *all* salespeople, not just bankers.

Why is prospecting feared so much? Because the fear of rejection is escalated to an alarm level. When dealing across the desk with someone who has come to the bank, the CSR or teller may feel somewhat uncomfortable if he or she cannot be of service. But, consider the feeling when you *initiate* the contact with a specific agenda in mind and then meet with rejection. All of a sudden, the entire day is ruined.

To ward off the likelihood of frequent rejection, even many good salespeople develop a temporary problem that may actually prevent them from making calls and setting appointments. This immobility is referred to in the industry as *call reluctance.* It can negatively affect people who want to be salespeople and who depend upon sales skills to survive. Think how easy it is for bankers to develop call reluctance when we don't want to sell to begin with and we're on salary.

HOW TO PROSPECT

Like any other difficult task, prospecting becomes easier if you break it down into its component parts. Think about the outside call as a four-step process.

1. Pre-call planning
2. Making contact
3. Making the call
4. Follow up

Let's examine each step individually.

Pre-Call Planning

In preparing to make a quality call, there are several key questions you can use to ensure its success. And by the way, we recommend that only quality calls be counted. If you drop by a customer's place of business on the way back from lunch just to say hello, there may be some value in that, but it does not qualify as a quality call. This is not to say that in some smaller communities an unannounced visit cannot be valuable.

A bank we know made this mistake: The CEO decided to concentrate on *quantity* in this $100 million bank in Texas. He required his officers to make 20 calls per week. That, of course, was impossible and the officer call program was instituted, not followed, and then dropped all within a six-week period. There is simply no way that 20 *quality* calls can be made weekly by someone who also holds a full-time job doing other things.

Here is a suggested pre-call checklist.

1. **What is the purpose of the call?** While there are many purposes, most calls are designed to do one or more of the following:

   - Cement a present relationship.
   - Enhance a present relationship.
   - Initiate a preliminary new business relationship seeking information on a prospect's needs (building rapport).
   - Acquaint the prospect with a new product or service.

   The key point is to know exactly what the purpose or purposes are.

2. **What is known about the customer?** If you call on an existing customer, much information should be available. Be very familiar with file information. If you call on a new prospect, make every effort to find out information about the customer. You can use Dun and Bradstreet information, facts from previous calls and other resources to prepare for the call.

   Preparation is critical for these reasons:

- It builds confidence for the calling officer.
- The prospect will be impressed knowing that the banker has taken the time to prepare for the meeting.

3. **What potential needs could the customer have that the bank might be able to meet?** Depending upon the purpose of the call and what you know about the customer, you can easily list anticipated needs and ways to meet them.

Making Contact

This second stage of prospecting concerns ways to properly contact the prospect. Generally there are two ways to proceed—by phone and by mail. Which one you use and in what order depends largely upon the nature of the relationship. Consider these three possible scenarios.

Scenario 1. If the prospect is a present customer well known to the bank, then usually a simple phone call to set an appointment will be sufficient. Normally the purpose of the phone call is to merely set the appointment. The appointment, not a sale, is the call's objective. As the banker, you should introduce yourself, establish rapport, explain briefly the reason for the call and suggest a possible appointment time and date. Here are some do's and don'ts.

Do's	Don'ts
• Smile (it shows even over the phone)	• Ramble
• Be sincere	• Be negative
• Be prepared	• Talk to wrong person
• Be enthusiastic	• Be pushy

Scenario 2. If you don't know the prospect (a cold call) then we suggest that the first step is a letter to the prospect. The components of an effective letter include:

- An initial brief statement
- A suggested product (when applicable)

FIGURE 7.1   Sample Letter

Ms. Sandi Mitchell
President
Innovation Corp.
111 W. Main Street
Middle America, USA

Dear Ms. Mitchell,

Please allow me to introduce our bank, First American, to you and your company. My name is Charlene Gaffney and I'm Vice President and a loan officer. As you may know, our bank specializes in lending to small businesses.

Would a working capital line of credit make sense to you? We have recently introduced a secured line of credit which many companies like yours are finding beneficial.

Would it be possible for me to meet personally with you to discuss how we might be of service? I'll call you next week to see if we can find a mutually agreeable time to meet.

Thank you for your consideration.

Very truly yours,

Charlene Gaffney

- A request for an appointment
- A promise to follow up

Figure 7.1 shows a sample letter.

The follow-up phone call then should be made as we discussed in the first scenario.

Scenario 3.   One of a banker's most treasured gifts is that of a referral. Perhaps the referral comes from another department of the bank or from a director. Perhaps the referral is from another customer. Assuming that the prospect is not already a bank customer, the initial contact will most likely follow Scenario 1.

But referrals are also unique in many respects. For example, the person making the referral often knows some valuable information about the prospect such as a specific need for a product or service or a cause for dissatisfaction at another financial institution. The information might also concern the nature of the business, the temperament of the individual or the age, marital status, etc. The more information you have, the better your chances of a successful sales call.

But perhaps the most valuable aspect of a referral is its "warming" effect. By that we mean that a referral often turns a cold call into a warm prospect. Having someone refer your bank to a customer is a high compliment. Turning a referral into a personal introduction may pave the way for immediate success whereas most prospecting is a long-term process. One word of caution: Always ask permission to use the name of the person who referred you.

If referrals are so nice to have, why do some bankers get so few and some so many? The obvious answer might be a difference in service quality. But assuming relative parity on the service front, the major reason why some bankers receive more referrals than others is that they *ask*. That's right, they develop a habit of asking for referrals from present customers. Here are some typical examples.

- "Now that we've got this IRA completed, Mr Wylie, is there someone else in your family or at your office who might appreciate knowing about our product?"
- "We appreciate this corporate checking account, Mrs. Merk, now would any of the other corporate officers or employees have needs that we could handle?"
- "Jim, we appreciate the opportunity to handle this home equity loan request. The money for your daughter's education will be well spent. Do you know any other parents in your situation who might benefit from our home equity line of credit?"

The possibilities are endless. What it takes to be successful at getting referrals is to develop a habit of asking. What it takes to convert referred prospects to relationships is an acquired skill we call prospecting. Read on for how to handle the prospect face to face.

Seeing the Customer on His or Her Turf: Making the Call

After you've been in banking for a time, the idea of meeting someone new at the office is not intimidating. But going to the office of a prospect, especially someone you don't know, is not easy. Finding the time to go (procrastination) is a problem. Lack of self-confidence and not enough preparation are all obstacles. But let's assume that all obstacles have been overcome and you are about to walk in the door to meet the prospect. What sequence of events should occur? What should you do?

The Opening.   It should go without saying that you should be on time and perhaps ten minutes early. Get a feel for the place of business. Notice plaques or awards in the reception area. Thumb through any trade magazines that might be in the reception area. You're looking for items that will help you establish rapport. That's right, here's that rapport word again. Because, you see, once you get to the prospect's place of business or home, the sales call takes on the same sequence as one taking place in your office, with a few deviations. Building rapport is even more important because there is no existing relationship as we assumed in Chapters 3 through 6.

Another reason to arrive early is so that you can review either your handwritten notes or call sheet. Be sure you know the purpose of the visit and a list of questions you may want to ask.

When you are introduced to the prospect, be sure to note the secretary's or receptionist's name. Knowing your prospect's key employees will be valuable in the long run. As you are introduced, be sure to give your name and the name of your bank. Thank the prospect for taking time to meet with you. Rapport building is then critical. One of our favorite techniques is to begin a conversation with something of interest in your prospect's office or home. Noticing the pictures on the walls, the awards or trophies or pictures of family gives you an immediate insight into what is important to the prospect. If you can discover some common bond between you and the customer— both avid golfers or concerned parents or interested in Oriental art—then your chances for a successful call are improved.

The key to establishing rapport is asking questions. You are seeking information that can assist you in helping the customer in the future. Encourage the customer to talk about personal interests. If you have a referral, then perhaps a discussion of a mutual acquaintance could break the ice. This warm-up period can be short or extended. Take your lead from the prospect. Some of them want to get to the bottom line, no wasted time. Others are delighted to talk about themselves and their interests for several minutes.

The Transition.   At some point in the conversation it will become appropriate to move from rapport building to the agenda you have in mind. The transition process takes practice but it usually begins either when you are asked why you're there or you feel that it is time to talk about that. Transition phrases may be similar to these:

- "Mr. Kunkel, as you know our bank has a reputation for specializing in loans to middle market companies such as yours. My purpose today is to discover more about your business and to find out how we can earn the right to be of service."
- "I really appreciate your telling me about your unique family, but I don't want to take too much of your time, so, if I may, I'd like to tell you specifically why I'm here."

The key point to remember is to make as natural a segue as possible from the initial rapport building segment into the purpose of the meeting.

The Purpose.   In the main portion of the call to a new prospect, you may have a specific product or service in which the prospect may have indicated an interest. At this point, it may be appropriate to explain it to the prospect, encourage feedback and proceed in whatever manner seems appropriate.

But more than likely, the purpose of a call on a new prospect is information gathering. As a result the next steps are precisely those we've discussed in the preceding chapters: qualifying, presenting, handling objections and gaining commitment. In the initial call, the qualifying or needs assessment phase will often be the only appropriate objective. Here's how we recommend that you conduct the interview.

Get the prospect talking. The way you learn about the prospect's business and its needs is by asking questions and then listening. Typical open-ended phrases such as these are sure to elicit appropriate responses:

- "Mr. Hinkle, it certainly appears that you have done a fine job of building this company. How long has the company been in business and why was it begun?"
- "Exactly what does the company do and what is your strategy in maintaining growth and profitability?"
- "Tell me about your background and how you came to be doing what you're doing now."
- "What do you expect from your bank? How are those needs being met? What would our bank need to do to earn the right to serve your needs?"

Prior to the meeting you should have developed other questions to gain information about the customer. We recommend that you take appropriate notes throughout the interview. This is not an interrogation; it is a conversation. But you can take pertinent notes—they will prove invaluable during the follow-up portion of the call.

During some initial calls, you may have an opportunity to suggest possible solutions to the prospect's needs. But, here again, it is important not to be pushy. Remember that your goal is primarily information gathering. You will have the opportunity to present solutions at a later time using the methods learned in Chapter 4.

Figure 7.2 illustrates a sample chart to help you keep track of your prospecting.

Finishing the Call. Don't overstay your appointed time unless the prospect specifically asks you to stay. But be sure that before the meeting concludes the next step is agreed upon. Fix responsibility for future actions. Is there a next move and if so, whose is it? Although many outcomes are possible, two are most common. One outcome is when no relationship is apparent (or desired) in the immediate future. Your responsibility as

FIGURE 7.2   Telephone Marketing/Prospecting Score Sheet

TELEPHONE MARKETING/PROSPECTING
TELEPHONE ACTIVITY AND RESULTS SCORE SHEET

Name _____   Company _____

Date							
Day	Mon.	Tue.	Wed.	Thu.	Fri.	Sat.	Total
Hour of the Day							
Hours Phoning							
Attempts							
Contacts							
Appointments							
Sales							
Drop Bys							
Not Interested							
Call Backs							
Not In–Future Follow-Up							
Busy Signals							
Wrong Numbers							
Referrals							
Must Talk to Other Person							
Miscellaneous							
Total							

(My total/attempts/contacts/results/appointments and/or referrals.)

My performance evaluation relates to the percentages of my results and what I will do to improve those results: _____

_____

_____

_____

_____

_____   Date: _____

Source: McCuistion and Associates and Thom Norman.

a calling officer is then limited to recording the results of the call and sending a letter of appreciation to the prospect.

The hoped-for outcome, though, is one that requires a more promising follow-up.

The Follow-Up

If there appears to be a high level of interest in establishing a relationship, then merely reporting on the call and sending an appropriate letter is obviously not enough. The talented calling officer will develop a specific proposal for the prospect, and eventually convert the prospect to a relationship. This process can take days, weeks, months and even years. The follow-up process never ends. Bankers must continue to help to maintain the relationship.

Sales and marketing executives claim the average sale is made after the fifth call. That does not mean aggressive telephone bombardment. It does mean keeping in touch via note or sending new information. It means staying in touch so the customers know you're there and willing to help.

WHO ARE THE PROSPECTORS?

This chapter would be incomplete without some mention of who should be the calling officers. Should every officer call? What about directors? And what role should CSRs, tellers and back office personnel take? Let's examine each group briefly.

Directors

Most directors have neither the time, talent or inclination to make sales calls. As you'll read in the chapter on directors, the best hope is for "actionable leads." Directors can and, in most cases, should be alert to potential customer contacts. Some banks, such as the well-run and profitable Marathon National Bank in Los Angeles, prefer to keep directors out of the business development function altogether. But many community banks encourage directors to give leads on a continuing basis.

CEO

In many community banks and, to some extent, in larger banks as well, the CEO may be the main prospector. We continue to believe that this is appropriate especially for large and influential customers. We also encourage CEOs to take other officers along on the calls. It's great experience for them and the CEO can delegate follow-up activities.

Managers, Supervisors, Lenders

Not everyone in this group should become a prospector for two reasons:

1. Many are old-time bankers, set in their ways, negative on selling and will not change. Why send out someone who may be a liability rather than an asset?
2. Some are not qualified to call on certain accounts. Sending a cashier or new-accounts supervisor to call on a potential loan customer is not smart. Instead, if the officers have calling skills, let them call on existing customers and emphasize services and products in their respective areas of expertise.

Commercial loan officers and marketing officers are particularly well suited to call on business accounts. Longtime Plano, Texas banker Linn Bleggi has new accounts, lending and marketing skills and is an effective business recruiter for Team Bank. She, like many others in her position, benefits from experience as well as her knowledge of the community.

More and more we see branch managers with the title of branch sales manager. Prospecting skills are a necessary part of the job description.

Customer Contact Personnel

Most CSRs and tellers are not actively involved in making outside calls on non-customers. But here's an idea as to how they can be proactive customers: Don Stricklin, president of Bank One, Abilene, Texas, has his tellers call daily two of their customers they helped that day. The caller thanks them for their business, checks on customer satisfaction and offers to be of service in the future. Great idea, and it can be done with CSRs as well.

Back-Office Personnel

Here again we seldom see prospecting by back-office employees. But they should be alert to situations that might lead to existing customer dissatisfaction. While most situations can be handled on the spot, there may be times when a referral to an officer could mean saving a valuable relationship by smoothing over the problem. And one prospecting idea might be a periodic review of endorsements on incoming deposit items or other transit items to identify where non-customers are banking. This information can be relayed to the appropriate source and added to prospect file information.

SUMMARY

Prospecting is the first step in soliciting non-customer business. And it's the most feared because of the possibility of rejection. It is also avoided because calling on prospects takes valuable time away from a banker's busy day.

You can prospect successfully with adequate pre-call planning and preparation. Knowing the purpose of your call and obtaining background on the prospect increases the likelihood of a successful call. In most instances a successful prospecting call means that you built rapport and gathered information.

Follow-up is extremely important as successful culmination of a relationship requires ongoing contact and weeks, months or even years of work.

CHAPTER 8

Selling and the Board of Directors

"Our board of directors has adopted a written marketing plan which fixes responsibility for its implementation with top management and includes such items as cross-selling by customer personnel."

CHARLES E. MARTIN, PRESIDENT/CEO
First American Bank
Pelham, Alabama

THE BOARD OF DIRECTORS

This book is primarily designed for banks and other financial institutions with assets under $250 million. In larger banks the functions of board members may be somewhat different and this may apply to some smaller banks as well. The major criterion for utilizing the portions of this book that relate to board members is this: The CEO and board members themselves must be committed to participating in the marketing/sales function and changing to a sales culture or enhancing an existing one.

In other words, where the board is either too old, too conservative or too disinterested then ignore the portions of this book that relate to its beneficial use. Instead, concentrate on the CEO and other members of the team. We hope the board will at least see fit to reward those who do make solid contributions to profitability and increased customer satisfaction.

Our hope, however, mirrors our experience in working with boards in strategic planning and in seminar presentations. Our belief is this:

■ ■ ■

Most board members are willing to assist in the marketing and sales effort which we commonly refer to as "business development."

■ ■ ■

Four reasons that many board members are ineffective in this area are:

1. Many of them fail to understand the importance of their contribution.
2. Many have never, or at least not on a consistent basis, been asked to help.
3. Many don't really know how to help.
4. Everyone has significant time constraints.

How can these four problems be overcome? Reading this book will help on points one, two and three. Designing a simple, but consistent business development program with board assistance and input will enhance point three. Utilizing focused and limited time commitments along with measuring achievements will help to solve point four. Bank directors by and large can be of most benefit in two specific areas: involvement in strategic planning and the providing of actionable leads.

THE DIRECTOR AND STRATEGIC PLANNING

We firmly believe that the single most important thing a bank can do to ensure its long-term viability is to begin or enhance its strategic planning process. Notice we said "process" because planning must go on at all times in order to stay on the cutting edge of change and maintain an edge over present and future competitors.

An essential part of any strategic planning process is to ask and answer at least these questions:

- What business are we in?
- What products/service should we be offering?
- What markets should we be serving?

Directors bring years of experience and maturity to their jobs. Many don't know as much about banking as they would like but they usually have pertinent input in the following areas:

- What does the community want in a bank?
- What areas are not being properly serviced?
- What is the bank's image in the community?
- What new products and services could be discussed and/or implemented?
- What level of customer service is being provided?

Annual planning sessions designed to include marketing discussions can be very beneficial in reinforcing a bank's goal of being customer-driven. An effective board can not only review past results but also make informed suggestions for innovative changes.

Here are some specific suggestions on how to include marketing and sales strategies into the strategic planning process.

THE DIRECTOR AND "ACTIONABLE LEADS"

In many banks, especially newly chartered and smaller ones, directors are expected to be a constant source of new business development. And in the euphoria of a newly opened bank, many directors are both interested and effective in bringing in deposits and referring friends, family and associates to the bank. But as a bank matures the initial enthusiasm seems to wane and CEOs constantly tell us two important facts:

1. They still want directors to participate in business development.

2. It is difficult if not impossible to make that happen on a consistent basis.

So what should we do? The answer depends, of course, on several factors including the board makeup itself. Bob Dye of Gary-Wheaton Bank, N.A., located in the western Chicago suburbs tells of having worked with a board whose average age was in the 80s. To expect strong business development (or very much else for that matter) might be overly optimistic. One bank we worked with consisted solely of executive officers plus two very nice but ineffective elderly ladies who had no ability or interest in being involved in marketing.

Getting board involvement depends, too, on the CEO. Many CEOs just do not want to spend the time to nurture directors' interest in business development tasks. If, as in many banks, the board chairman merely presides at meetings, then lack of CEO prodding will spell certain ineffectiveness.

Finally, there are banks in which the CEO merely regards the board involvement as a bother at best and a nuisance at worst. Previous directors we've worked with had a desire to bring in only business which personally benefitted them or which was so marginal that the director lost interest after several referrals led to unsatisfactory relationships.

Because of the above-mentioned problems we suggest using board members primarily for obtaining actionable leads. We first heard the term *actionable leads* from Bob Dye when he was working for the respected consulting firm Financial Shares Corporation in Chicago. What the term means to us is that directors can be involved in a time effective manner if their bank merely sets up a consistent system of asking for leads. Good leads may include the following:

• An individual over whom the director has some influence. Typically this might include relatives, business associates, customers and suppliers of the director's business and certain personal friends and acquaintances.

• An individual or business owner who has expressed either dissatisfaction with present banking relationships or an interest in banking with your bank.

- An individual or business owner who is specifically targeted by the bank as a top banking prospect. Unlike the leads that can be generated from the two previous sources, this method may require the director to write a letter or make a call either by phone or in person.

GETTING ACTION

Getting the director to supply actionable leads should not be difficult. It can be done by at least the following methods:

- Create a contest among board members wherein each board member's leads (or lack of them) are discussed at each monthly board meeting. We suggest that board members be grouped in teams to create a competitive environment and to bring as much peer pressure to bear as possible.
- Set up a breakfast, luncheon or customer seminar where directors can invite their prospects to attend with them. There is a special attraction if a director can do something for prospective customers other than just refer names to bank officers.

Many directors lose interest, however, where there is no action. We recommend that leads be assigned by the CEO and the marketing manager to appropriate officers. Those officers must take action. By action we mean, of course, customer contact.

Earlier in this book we outlined specific ways to take that action. But for now, let us merely emphasize the necessity for the prospects being called on within a short period of time following referral.

THE REPORTING

When the calling officer has taken action, the process is still not yet complete. The circle doesn't close until the director providing the actionable lead receives a report from the calling officer on the action taken and the results of the action. Reporting serves at least three purposes:

1. It forces the officer to actually make the call.
2. It leaves a paper trail for future follow-up by bank personnel and provides valuable information in getting the business in the future.
3. Most importantly, the director receives timely feedback on the results of an action taken. We believe that the reporting will encourage both follow-up by the director and the future provision of other actionable leads.

SUMMARY

In many community banks a function of boards of directors is to develop new business and cement current relationships. Most directors have time problems and limited expertise in selling specific bank services. But with some direction and monitoring at board meetings, the directors can be encouraged to give the officers leads on which action can be taken. Early follow-up by the calling officer and a written report on the results are essential to board success.

CHAPTER 9

Selling and the CEO

"Managing in today's bank...means meeting the leadership challenges brought on by deregulation— improving employee performance, developing market- driven products, developing a responsive and flexible organizational structure, increasing productivity, improving service quality, and developing a sales culture, to name just a few. It means producing change and managing the effects of change."

JAMES H. DONNELLY, JR., AND STEVEN J. SKINNER
The New Banker

The focal point of any sales culture mandates that the CEO be committed and involved. The CEO is the leader—the cheerleader—the head marketeer. The CEO should be the example from which the organization takes it lead. *The New Banker*, a book by James H. Donnelly, Jr., and Steven J. Skinner from which the above quote is taken, is recommended reading for every community bank CEO and manager.

A NEW BREED

The CEO of the 1990s will be a new breed. The CEO will be management and marketing driven, will have a passion for superior customer service and innovation and will not be satisfied with less than optimum earnings. Here are two bits of good news:

1. Not all of today's CEOs will be replaced, but they will change.
2. If our predictions are fulfilled and our program carried out, the bottom line will be even better than before.

When we say "better than before" we imply that those who choose to implement this program are already top performers. Our experience is that the banks and other financial institutions at the top of the industry are the ones who are constantly trying to be just that tiny bit better. As a result, many of today's top performers are already part of the new breed. This survival guide for top performers will merely provide another way to get the job done.

For those readers who are mentally prepared to excel in the Nineties, but who are looking for the vehicle, we believe this is it.

The CEO Challenge

The role of CEO in tomorrow's financial institution will require meeting at least these challenges:

1. The board of directors must be sold on the need for a customer driven culture. (See the preceding chapter for ideas on how to do that.)
2. The CEO's management team and staff must be shown, by example, how a commitment to helping the customer produces a motivated team, loyal customer base, more income opportunities for employees and a blacker bottom line.
3. Some CEOs must shed a portion of their present duties to make room for their role as chief marketing officer.

Selling the Board of Directors

Among all the groups involved in the sales culture, the CEO has a singularly unique task. That task is convincing those above and below that the marketing/sales effort is not only essential but that the CEO's involvement must be hands on. This is not an easy task, particularly if the board is entrenched in the past. Some boards are simply cosmetic and, in those circumstances, can be virtually ignored. For active boards the previous chapter should be required reading.

For the CEO who can do nothing to motivate a tired board but who would like the enthusiasm of an advisory group, we would suggest consideration of an advisory board or business development board. With today's potential personal liability for board members, it may actually be easier to recruit community leaders for an advisory position.

THE ADVISORY BOARD

One of the Southwest's premier bankers is the now-retired J. Don Wright. During his tenure at the helm at the former Lakewood Bank and Trust in Dallas (now First Interstate), Don was a pioneer in putting together an active business advisory board. As the bank's CEO he assumed personal responsibility for its formation and its activities. The author of two excellent books on boards of directors' responsibilities, Don utilized aggressive business people who not only saw fit to bank with him, but who were actively involved in referring new business to the bank.

Many CEOs try to delegate responsibility for an advisory board to another senior officer. Sometimes that works. But our recommendation is that direct, personal contact between CEO and board member be maintained. Components of forming a successful advisory board include:

- Identification of aggressive business people
- Design of an action program to involve them (luncheons, seminars, business cards, calling programs)

- Interaction with regular board members to share insights and to recruit advisory board performers to regular board membership

In all other activities, CEO personal involvement is critical.

MOTIVATING THE TEAM

Two of the acknowledged traits of leaders are vision and communication skills. An effective CEO needs both. Vision is needed to enable the CEO to paint successful and vivid pictures in the minds of other management and staff personnel. Essentially, we recommend that CEOs do all or part of the following:

Self-education.   It won't be surprising that we recommend that CEOs know the materials in this book forward and backward. There are also excellent materials in today's marketplace that provide the dedicated CEO with additional perspective. In particular, we recommend the following five books. (Complete entries are shown in the Bibliography.)

1. *Bankers Who Sell*
2. *Thriving on Chaos*
3. *The New Banker*
4. *Service America*
5. *Marketing Financial Services*

Coaching/managing.   We envision the CEO's job as the chief marketing manager, not the chief salesperson. What that means in simple terms is that the CEO must develop strategies and tactics to achieve the bank's volume and profit goals. That's the easy part. The difficult part is that the *team* must do the work. The CEO's success will largely depend upon the ability to recruit good people, train and coach them and provide an atmosphere in which team members will succeed. It is the CEO who is ultimately accountable, the one who shoulders the blame for any lack of success but who must share the credit for all the accomplishments.

We recommend that a CEO spend a minimum of a week in a well-structured management course to refresh skills and introduce new concepts of dealing with people. The CEO must understand that getting present employees to change is the most important and the most difficult goal. Behavioral change occurs over time. The CEO should schedule a two-hour or three-hour meeting with key managers to introduce the sales culture strategy. One of the main objectives should be, not just to disseminate information, but rather to enlist the help and support of the management team.

THE "HELP ME, HELP US, HELP THEM" MEETING

Our experience is that many CEOs who both recognize the need for a sales culture and want to make changes simply don't because they don't know what to do. We've already mentioned the first two steps—getting mentally ready and personally educated and getting the board involved. Next, involve management and staff. Effectively, the successful CEO must sell the rest of the organization on the importance of establishing and maintaining a customer-driven marketing and sales environment. This is not an event. It is a *process*, a commitment to fundamentally alter how banking is done in the organization. And, it is not to be taken lightly. It demands planning and follow-up, involvement and rewards. Change is almost never easy, but in this case, it is necessary.

The CEO should already have been providing management and staff with articles, books, videos, etc., to spark interest in the marketing approach. Especially we recommend that you hold a meeting with the other management personnel from the executive vice president down to the head bookkeeper and head teller. The purposes of the meeting should be clearly stated prior to and in the meeting. You may choose to use a capable in-house marketing person or hire outside sales consultants but, in any case, the CEO must be the key mover and shaker. Convey a clear and serious message.

The Goal

The CEO needs help. The CEO needs commitment. How does this occur? Two ways: involvement and asking for help. The management team must buy into the change and the best way to achieve that, in our opinion, is to involve them in designing the change. How do you do that? Read on.

The Agenda

As in most meetings, the better the agenda, the more productive the meeting. Involving the team in building the agenda can be an effective start. Consider sending a brief memo to each participant (See Figure 9.1).

The agenda can be drawn from these responses but it should include as a minimum the following two parts:

1. Opening remarks by the CEO as to the goals to be accomplished at the meeting and the necessity for achieving them.
2. Discussion by the team and agreement upon the goals to be gained from a culture change; a proposed timetable; and specific assignments for getting the process started. This portion requires that goals and timetables be reduced to writing and disseminated to everyone after the meeting.

To facilitate this meeting is critical. Everyone must feel the freedom to contribute and to be a part of the plan itself. Sometimes this concept is referred to as "ownership."

AND NOW FOR THE HARD PART

The excitement of conceiving a new way of viewing things, the euphoria of a well-designed and successful meeting can quickly turn into depression when your plan must evolve into implementation and follow-up. Momentum is important; you may lose it if you allow deadlines to slip or other "more impor-

FIGURE 9.1 Sample Memo

TO: Management/Sales Team
FROM: Your CEO/Sales Manager
SUBJECT: Initial Sales Culture Change Meeting

You are cordially invited to attend a meeting to be held on Tuesday, January 5, at 3:00 P.M. in the board room. Its purpose is to discuss and outline a process by which our bank reaffirms its commitment to its customers, employees, community and shareholders by analyzing an organization driven by an exceptional desire to provide the very best quality products and services.

You undoubtedly recognize that the above goal, as well as our corporate mission statement, can only be achieved with the aid of *everyone* in the bank. This includes you and me and the custodian and security guard and everyone in-between. While I have some rather well-defined ideas as to how we should proceed, your help is requested.

Specifically, by noon on December 31, I will expect to receive from you, in writing, the following:
1. What items would you suggest for the agenda?
2. Please share with me your thoughts on these items:
   - Do we need to be more customer or marketing driven? Why or why not?
   - What are the *two* major obstacles we need to overcome in order to achieve our goals?
   - How, specifically, can each of these obstacles be overcome?
   - Please recommend ways in which *all* of our employees can be a part of making this change happen.
   - What specific ways can the bank or I help *you* in this transition?

---

tant" items to get in the way. Our best advice: You, as the CEO, are the only one who can refuse to allow your goals to be compromised. Everyone else on your staff can, and many will, find various excuses as to why this or that cannot be accomplished on time. Your commitment must be uncompromising. *In some ways this culture change may be the most difficult task you've ever taken on.* Because it will determine your bank's ability to survive profitably in the future, we believe it will also be your most important task. Showing you how is not nearly as difficult as convincing you why!

Included in the CEO's tasks are all areas of marketing such as these:

- Research customer needs
- Design new products and services to meet those needs
- Advertise new products and services
- Train present and future employees in selling skills
- Manage the marketing and sales functions

This book focuses primarily on the training of people in *how* and *why* to sell. Other segments of the program are detailed in the Bibliography listed at the end of the book. Or you may wish to hire professionals in those areas. We believe that the most difficult of the bank's tasks relates to the selling part of the marketing process.

As you read through this book you'll see how, by redefining *selling* as *helping*, the job of converting existing employees into "helpers" becomes not only possible, but actually simple. Simple is not to be confused with easy. Overcoming the reasons why bankers don't presently sell is not easy. But, as you'll see, it is much easier when you know the obstacles.

SUMMARY

The CEO of the future will be part of a new breed. He or she will be the bank's chief marketing officer, the one primarily charged with developing the vision and plan, communicating the vision and plan within the organization and following up to ensure successful implementation. An appropriate strategy, one that involves many key staff members, will make the job easier. Though the marketing process is multifaceted, this book places primary emphasis on the sales process. CEO leadership is essential to making the sales culture a reality.

CHAPTER 10

Managers, Supervisors and Lenders

Installing a sales culture and becoming customer-driven cannot be done without the commitment of the management team and lenders. And, if you're like thousands of bankers we've surveyed, you really don't want to sell, do you? In fact, many of you have told us that one of the reasons you're in banking is that you don't have to sell. Interestingly enough, otherwise successful programs can be consciously or unconsciously torpedoed by middle and top management because they resist the idea of selling.

HOW TO GET YOUR PROGRAM OFF THE GROUND

We will repeat many times our belief that the implementation is the most difficult part of the process. Without committed management, no plan regardless of how well conceived can succeed. The real question is this: What will it take to gain the commitment of this group?

Take this short quiz. After you answer the four questions you might be surprised at how your thinking may change.

1. Are you sincerely interested in helping your customers?
2. Are you interested in developing your employees' potential and helping them to prosper?

3. Do you personally want to increase your income? (This is a tough one.)
4. Do you want to help your bank grow and prosper?

We bet that most of you answered yes to all four questions. And further, we wager that you're presently doing an admirable job in each category. So the real question is, How can we do it even better?

First, Keep an Open Mind

You, yourself, are likely to be concerned about change. You may be skeptical about whether the program can get off the ground. If you prejudge the proposed change, if your staff even senses that you disapprove or are skeptical, the program itself faces an uphill battle from the start. One of the management's most important jobs is to keep an open mind to any new idea. Heaven knows, banking has had so many changes in the last few years, change itself should come as no surprise.

Second, Respond Positively to your CEO's Requests

If you are asked to provide input or questions or agenda items, then, by all means, do so. When your boss requests something, don't you normally comply? In the case of sales, however, we're frankly requesting that you "accentuate the positive, eliminate the negative." Why? How often are you successful at something you don't like to do? Not often, we'll surmise. So, bottom line, do not prejudge the program from a negative perspective. Remember if it doesn't "take," it's your responsibility, too. Being a good follower is just as important as being a good leader.

Third, Volunteer To Lead the Way

Now some of you are probably thinking, "The pair who wrote this book are nuts. Why should I volunteer to take a proactive stance in something I don't even enjoy doing?" We understand. But what if we can convince you that:

- the benefits far outweigh the costs and
- you *do* like to do it?

That's what we believe will happen when you've finished this book.

Fourth, Be an Ardent Supporter of Board and CEO Initiatives

In other words, even if you don't like it and won't participate and volunteer, do your best anyway because you're supposed to. Here's an example:

> In many seminars, especially for lending personnel, the question is asked, "How many of you enjoy working with insurance?" Out of thousands of bankers only one person has ever replied affirmatively. When we asked her why she liked working with insurance, she simply replied, "Because it's my job."

AFTER COMMITMENT, THEN WHAT?

Participation. None of you reading this book will find the subject of bankers who need selling skills to be a new one. Unless we miss our guess, most of you have attended several conferences over the years where the subjects of marketing, cross-selling and customer service have been prominently discussed. Then, depending upon whether you were positively or negatively inclined to the ideas, you may have found yourself offering some of the familiar excuses you'll see here.

"It's Not My Job"

Do you recognize yourself here? See if you've ever said these to yourself.

- "Sure, selling is important—but I'm a loan officer. That's not my job."

- "Sure, customer service is essential—but my staff is strictly back office. That's not my job."
- "Oh, yes, I know that calling on prospective customers is important, but I'm too busy managing the credit and loan department. That's not my job."
- "Selling? Are you kidding? I'm the cashier. That's not my job."

Sound familiar? We thought so! It's an all too easy trap to fall into. But consider your answers to these two questions:

1. Are you in a position in the bank where either you and/or your employees are involved in helping the customer meet financial needs?
2. Are you and/or your employees in a job of finding ways to increase your bottom line by profitably providing products, services or ideas to your customers?

Frankly, we can't think of a job in the bank, from the janitor to the auditor to the collection department that can answer no to these two questions. And guess what, if you answer yes to either one, *it is your job*!

"I Don't Have Time"

Ever said this or heard someone else say, "I really would

- make my calls
- cross-sell services
- qualify my customers better
- manage my employees more effectively
- smile more often
- be more empathetic, etc.

. . .if only I had the time"? Guess what? You've got all the time there is. The real question here is: Is there anything more worthy of our time than helping our customers?

Not having enough time is usually a cop-out, especially for managers. Perhaps your delegation skills need some honing. Or, perhaps your bank, like so many others today, has decided to improve the bottom line by cutting costs. Read on.

"We Can't Afford It"

Ever hear these before?

- "We would do a better job of cross-selling but we're really running lean and mean right now."
- "We had to cut expenses so our marketing person had to go."
- "We really need to hold down costs so let's cut our training budget" or . . . "Let's trim our hours" or . . . "Let's eliminate some of our advertising."

Now we aren't so naive as to think that there aren't times when those excuses make sense. But have you ever been to a major hotel that eliminated its bell captain or canceled its 800 number? Or to a dry-cleaner who quit using plastic bags? Or to a grocery store who began using only plastic bags? Or to any business that employed untrained, incompetent, rude personnel to handle your needs? How did it make you feel?

In other words, your task as a manager/supervisor/officer is to get involved. No excuses. It's your job. Make the time. Spend the money. And, unless we're wrong, we think that you've got seminar materials, magazine articles and personal knowledge and ideas that can make significant contributions to the process.

WHAT YOU AND THE CEO HAVE IN COMMON

In the previous chapter we pointed out that the CEO's unique role was to sell those above him or her (the board) and those below (you). Your task is only slightly less difficult.

First, you must sell yourself. We've given you ample reasons to make that happen.

Second, you've got to become key team players with other colleagues as well as with those somewhat above or below you in the management hierarchy.

Third, you've got to become a salesperson yourself. This entire book is designed to help you do that.

Finally, you've got to train, challenge, lead and manage your people because more than likely they will meet and interact with more customers than you will.

So you and the CEO both have multiple challenges. This book does not contain specific sales *management* information. Depending upon your own personal background, you may need training in sales management.

YOUR MULTIPLE ROLES IN THE SALES CULTURE PROCESS

We've previously mentioned the need for your commitment and participation and why both are difficult but essential. However, the biggest challenge of all will be your role in driving the process down through the entire organization. One of the best ways to inspire those who work with you is your ability to lead by example. Yes, that's right. Someone will always be watching to see how you help the customer, what your attitude is towards superior service, what your performance is during incentive programs, what your ideas are for improving service quality and the bottom line. Yes, that's right. Your performance will be measured, both from above and from below.

Is this frightening? After all, if you wanted to be measured you'd have gone into sales, right? Ah, but you did go into sales. It's just that you didn't know it.

YOUR ROLE AS SERVICE PROVIDER

In community banks and many other financial institutions, lenders and managers are expected to personally handle the largest, and hence, perhaps the most important customers. What this means is simply that many of you are already service providers. You have the primary responsibility for the "care and feeding" of the customer. You are their account officer or personal contact. When your customers want something, or need to complain, they call you. You have the opportunity to maintain and enhance, or to lose, very important relationships.

Let's return to the first question we asked: Are you sincerely interested in helping your customers? Anyone who hasn't answered yes deserves to be unemployed. Of course you want to help your customers. But selling...well, that's different. Or is it? Remember that we've redefined selling to mean helping. So what we're really suggesting is that one way to help your customer is to increase the products or services for which the customer uses your bank. We are not talking about forcing, hard-selling or overly aggressive methods. Let's look at some examples of how specific bank opportunities arise.

THE LOAN OFFICER

Don't tell us! We know. Loan officers in today's banking climate have enough to do just making good loans and collecting them. But unless we miss our guess, most of you as part of your job responsibilities have the task of making outside calls on present and prospective customers. Additionally each loan officer has more or less periodic personal or telephone contact with customers. The point is this: Opportunities to help and expand customer relationships abound. Your job as a lender in today's bank includes your job as salesperson. Let's take a look at the reasons for this.

RELATIONSHIPS, RELATIONSHIPS, RELATIONSHIPS

If there was a buzzword of the 1980s in dealing with customers, it was *relationship banking*. The concept of relationship banking emerged as it became obvious that the cost of acquiring a new customer is higher than the cost of keeping an existing one. Additionally, many communities simply don't grow very much so the supply of new customers is small. Finally, studies have shown that the more services a customer uses within the bank, the more likely is the customer not to change banks. Here's where the importance of relationships comes in!

There's a compelling reason why loan officers should be concerned with relationships. We think you'll see the next three points as both obvious and powerful.

1. Relatively new relationships have a fear-of-the-unknown factor. The loan officer not only has to analyze the merits of the loan request, but also must be concerned about answers to questions such as these:

    *   What will the borrower do in times of distress?
    *   What unknown or concealed information about the customer will negatively impact repayment? This might include domestic or personal issues.
    *   What is the customer's ongoing relationship with other financial institutions and how might this impact our relationship?

2. Longtime customer relationships are more comfortable. That does not necessarily eliminate problems. In fact, many problem loans today are allowed to deteriorate precisely because we think we know our customers well and tend to be less vigilant. But the key point is that, over time, we've had the chance to observe our customers, to deal with them in good times and bad and to handle all types of services—checking and savings accounts for business and personal needs, traveler's checks, safety deposit boxes and perhaps even insurance and investments. We've had the opportunity to handle generational business, i.e., to service the children of our customers and to expand relationships in many directions. Lockbox and cash management accounts and trust services provide added benefits for the customer and more information for us.

3. How do we accumulate additional, valuable knowledge about newer customers without having to wait for years to pass? You guessed it! Help them use as many of our products and services as possible as soon as possible. How do we accomplish this? Right again! By understanding the helping (selling) process and making it a permanent part of who we are and what we do. Previous chapters have taken you through a step-by-step process in how to do it.

To sum up, by expanding new and existing relationships through a helping process you not only cement future profitable business but, by expanding your own insight into your customer's financial situation, you can increase your credit quality as well.

MANAGERS AND SUPERVISORS

Many of you are lending officers as well as managers so this section doubly applies to you. But specifically we want to address cashiers, new accounts and teller supervisors. Various other titled managers from executive and senior vice presidents to vice presidents and assistant vice presidents and assistant cashiers are included. Obviously the target group includes all officer-level staff such as banking officers.

Let's examine your role as service provider. Some of you have as your primary job accounting and administrative functions, which have little customer contact—and, more likely than not, you prefer it that way. We respect that. In fact, we sincerely believe that there are those whose jobs and/or personality will prevent them from being effective salespeople. So if this description fits you and if your boss agrees, here's what we suggest:

- Since you provide little direct customer service, we ask that, when you do, you approach it with this attitude: "I promise to be extremely courteous and professional to any customer because I will not get a second chance to have a continuing relationship to nurture." In other words, don't screw it up! The first rule in any relationship is do no harm. (Studies have shown that the cost to acquire a new customer is five times that of keeping an existing one!)
- Because you might be pressed into service more often than you think, we do recommend your study of this entire book. But there's another reason why your understanding of these concepts is important. You, by definition, are a critical part of the bank's team. Your CEO has committed to the sales culture and has requested your commitment as

well. Poor attitudes, negative remarks to your staff and peers can kill this culture change more quickly than almost anything else. Your *active* and *positive* assistance can ensure its success.

- Finally, your level of commitment will be observed by your CEO and your peers. And guess what we recommend in our consulting services to banks: If a key manager won't become a committed team player, and, in fact, tries consciously or subconsciously to sabotage the program, then you find a new team player. In other words, it's in your best interest. As the old cynic used to say about incentive programs, "Work real hard and you get to keep your job."

MANAGING TO MANAGE

Most of you will have dual roles of providing service and supervising people who do. Let's look closely at the critical management side of this issue. For some of you your role will be that of sales manager. In community banks, managers must lead by example. Your tellers or customer service reps are not likely to respond to training unless they see you as a bright, shining, consistent example. You are their leader, their cheerleader. But first, there are expectations to be communicated.

Whether or not you personally were involved in the design of a sales culture, it is your responsibility as a manager to make sure that your employees perform. Here are three steps you need to take:

1.   Whether meetings are called by you or by someone else, it is your primary responsibility to set the mood. "Beware, we're going to be indoctrinated by some sales guru," or "Look, just attend the meeting, this idea will blow over soon," can undermine the best of programs.
2.   In addition to not being negative about a sales culture, we think that your management expects you to actively support the effort. It may be up to you to assure your employees that there is no need for concern. You may be the one who must actively sell the concept to your employees. Yes,

we recognize that's difficult when you, yourself, have doubts about it. But this is an important part of a manager's job. You can do it.

3.   At some point, you, personally, must be sold on the concept of being customer-driven. When you buy into the program, when it becomes yours, all sorts of positive things will happen!

SUMMARY

The ultimate success of instilling a sales culture rests with management—those who have the dual responsibilities of helping the customers and managing the employees. The attitude and performance of managers and loan officers will be evaluated, not only by those for whom you work, but by those who work for you. Our philosophy is that everyone in the bank holds a job with an ultimate goal of helping customers succeed. Commitment or lack of commitment from management can make the process succeed or fail.

CHAPTER 11

Selling and Customer Contact Personnel

Good news! Many of you who are tellers, customer service reps (new accounts to you old-timers), loan secretaries, telephone operators and bookkeeping personnel who deal with customer complaints and questions are already doing a good job in sales. Some of you are in these jobs because you enjoy meeting people and helping them fulfill their financial needs. You've built a following of loyal customers who know you and call you by name; you know them as well. You are the bank to those people. And that's as it should be. Now let's explore how the job can be done even better.

THE "HEAD DOWN" PROBLEM

Did you ever walk into a store, need help and look around only to find the few people available had their heads down so you couldn't get their attention without feeling you were intruding? One of our speaker friends from Eau Claire, Wisconsin, Michael McKinley, has an entire presentation entitled, "Do I have to beg people to take my money?" To some extent that statement personifies the state of customer service in the world.

Sadly, the idea of "begging someone to take my money" applies to many of the banks in America today. In our own seminars and presentations for bankers, we use the "head down" analogy to refer to the callous disregard that many tellers and CSRs seemingly have for customers.

Do you work for a bank that isn't customer-driven? Take this short quiz and rate your institution.

- Do tellers and CSRs often have their heads down instead of showing an inviting appearance to customers?
- Does the atmosphere in your bank's lobby resemble that of a mausoleum?
- Do customers wait in long teller lines when other tellers are out to lunch or on break?
- Is your switchboard operator a robot or, even worse, a computer that spits out great customer service phrases such as "if you wish to speak to bookkeeping, punch 1" or "if you want to speak to a real person, please hang on and we'll try to find one."

Did you ever wonder how these things happen as a matter of course in some banks and not in others? Here's the good news: It's not the fault of customer contact personnel. It starts at the top, the very point we've been making throughout this book. Read the following true story as told to us by management consultant Jack Wilder.

Actions Speak Louder than Words

A bank CEO Jack knew called him and asked him to stop by and visit about a problem he was having. As Jack settled into a chair in the CEO's office, the CEO told Jack that he was experiencing a problem with his tellers, CSRs and secretarial staff. It seems that none of them was friendly to customers. "Head down" was the norm, no warmth, no calling of customers by name, no "hi, how are you" conversation.

The CEO wondered if Jack could help. Jack then suggested that the two of them station themselves close to the main entrance so he could observe what the CEO was talking about.

After about 15 minutes Jack said he thought he had it figured out and they returned to the office.

"See what I mean," said the CEO. "No one is friendly and it isn't because I haven't preached it to them often enough. What is causing my problem?"

"It's easy to see the problem—and its cause," said Jack. Looking straight at the CEO Jack said, "You're the problem."

"What do you mean?" asked the CEO.

"Simple," said Jack. "You are the leader, the role model. You and I stood by the door for 15 minutes. Not once during that time did *you* greet a customer or shake a hand or ask if you could be of service. Your people mirror what you do because your actions speak louder than words."

If this story sounds familiar, then read on—there is hope. It is difficult to launch and maintain a helpful customer-oriented program without leadership from the top.

CHANGING FROM MEDIOCRE TO SUPERIOR SERVICE

Ah, that work *change* again. Sometimes we think Webster's should define change this way: something that is difficult, something that is resisted.

So how does change in an organization occur? For those of you who are customer contact personnel such as tellers and CSRs, we do not believe that *you* can make it happen. We doubt that you can push a sales and customer-driven culture up the organization. But you *can* encourage the process.

CEO and Management Must Lead

As discussed in Chapters 9 and 10, we believe that changing cultures must begin at the top. So what can you do to encourage the process even if you have no power to change it?

If your management team hasn't read this book, give them a copy (charge it to the bank, of course).

Ask your supervisor what plans are being made to become more customer-oriented. If there are none, ask why. It may be ignorance of the need or, more likely, procrastination; or managers may be too busy putting out fires to concentrate on the need for change. The point is, you and your peers may be hampered by management from delivering competitive, quality products and services. You need to know why. After reading this book consider drafting a proposal to management. Your proposal should outline the benefits to both the bank and its customers, of a progressive sales-oriented culture and how it might be accomplished. Who knows, if it's good enough you might even be rewarded (don't get your hopes up!).

One more idea might be to discuss your ideas with others in order to win their support. Some of your peers will be negative (we bet you already know which ones), but many may support you if it becomes their idea also. In other words, try to gain consensus on the need for change and make the proposal "our proposal." There is strength in numbers.

WHY MANAGEMENT'S HELP IS ESSENTIAL

You may be thinking: Why should I worry about management? If they won't listen, I personally can raise the level of customer service to my customers. Obviously you can do this—and we applaud your attitude and encourage you to do so! Without a doubt, a terrific attitude combined with a sincere desire to help customers can become contagious. Other employees may notice you and follow your lead. Your supervisor may even notice and reward you with a raise, a promotion, You may even be the next vice president! Hey, this could happen!

On the other hand, your superior service and attitude may be perceived by your peers as a threat to their job security. Let's face it, some of your peers are a real liability. Some of them show up at work with a terrible attitude toward their family, their job, the customer and life in general. These people are poison to any positive culture.

So what does this have to do with management? Ask yourself who can change the attitudes of those few who can poison the culture. Also, do you truly believe that your hard work will be properly rewarded by a management that is not committed to the extent you are? We believe that many bank employees are former bank employees because their supervisors did not or would not provide the tools and support necessary to maintain the customer orientation essential in today's banking climate.

There's one other problem we've noticed in banks whose total team is not committed and that's the problem of caring for the internal customer. What do we mean by the "internal customer"? Let's use an example: Assume you are a CSR and a customer whose account you opened two weeks ago calls to determine whether or not his funds are available since he's heard nothing from the bank. You, as the customer contact person, ask him to hold while you call the appropriate person handling the transaction. The attitude of the employee you just called on the phone is one of these:

- "I don't have time for you."
- "Don't bother me with your problem."
- "Maybe I'll check it out and get back to you in a few hours."

Or you may simply get the information albeit grudgingly. Would you feel comfortable in transferring the customer to someone with that attitude? Ask yourself—are there certain employees or departments in your bank whom you simply do not trust to handle a customer properly? If you said yes, then what you have is a management problem, isn't it?

We simply believe that, without management's total commitment to the program, the best employees will either leave or be beaten down by lack of support and encouragement.

HOW TO MAKE GOOD "GREAT"

May we share a secret with you? The better banks are the ones who will use this book the most. Why? Because the way they become better banks is by doing that little bit extra to start with. With that in mind, let's assume that management wants to encourage you to be even better. What kinds of support should you expect?

Education

How many times have we said to bankers that education is a process, not an event? Has there ever been a time when the need for continuing education was more needed? And yet, many banks skimp here. And it's especially hard for community banks which normally lack a formal training function. We believe that there are two broad areas of education needed: product knowledge and service delivery.

Product Knowledge

Each bank has unique product needs. This book is not designed to address specific products. However, we want to make two important points here.

First—our experience indicates that most employees even in the better banks feel that they have inadequate product knowledge. They are unsure as to precisely what products and services are available, what their benefits are, who they are appropriate for, etc. This is the case even when bank management believes that it does a good job of providing information.

The second point builds on the first and was discussed in Chapters 3 through 7. The employee who feels inadequate in product knowledge will not be as effective in selling the product or service. It doesn't necessarily follow, though, that just knowing the products and services well will make an employee good at sales. It takes both product knowledge and sales skills. But the point is that product knowledge leads to confidence and confidence greatly assists an employee in helping the customer.

Service Delivery

This book concentrates on how to help (sell) the customer by providing very specific how-to steps in Chapters 3 through 7. Since most of the selling will be done by customer contact employees, those chapters are essential. They should be read, reread, studied, practiced and understood. They should be presented and practiced in a classroom setting with someone from inside or outside your bank until the principles become part of you. We promise that your customers will notice and that you will be noticed as well.

SUMMARY

The customer contact employee is ultimately the hands-on provider of products and services to customers. Changing to a sales culture is not easy and requires management commitment to a program that can be communicated throughout the organization. Finding ways to enhance present good practices is easier but it, too, requires each customer contact employee to keep an open mind to new ideas and to work diligently with management in cementing the customer-driven culture.

CHAPTER 12

Selling and Back Office Personnel

Yes, back office personnel must sell. That's the bad news. Here's the good news: selling means helping more in this area than anywhere else. This chapter explores the back office mentality and how to turn customers' problems into sales opportunities. We'll also relate the crucial roles that bookkeeping and customer service personnel play in the overall sales culture.

WHO ARE THESE PEOPLE IN THE BACK OFFICE?

We are using the term *back office* to refer to bank employees who normally do not spend most of their time in personal contact with the customer. This group varies from bank to bank but typically includes all or part of the following departments:

- Bookkeeping and accounting
- Auditing and loan review
- Trust operations
- Credit department

Why do we have the distinct impression that many of you will read this and automatically reject the notion that these groups have any connection whatsoever with sales? Perhaps you, like we, have worked with someone who has exhibited the stereotypical traits associated with the back office.

NUMBERS-ORIENTED PROBLEM SOLVERS

Would it surprise you to know that many people who deal with accounting data are numbers oriented? We hope not, because that's precisely what's required in many of these jobs. Money is a numbers business—we count it, we strap it and roll it, we account for it, we wire it, we balance it—in short, numbers are crucial to us and our customers. If you doubt the importance of being numbers oriented, consider this scenario.

Customer (on the phone):   "Hello, bookkeeping, yes this is Ima Outtabalance."

Bookkeeper: "Yes, Ms. Outtabalance, how may we be of service?"

Customer: "You people are sending my checks back and I need to know just exactly how much you show my balance to be."

Bookkeeper: "May I have your account number and date and amount of last deposit?"

Customer: "It's 25—1241—3 and I deposited $2,000 on January 4."

Bookkeeper: "OK, I have your account in front of me and, yes, I think that, uh, umm, all right, yes, you've got some money in the account."

Customer: "Well, how much?"

Bookkeeper: "Well, you know, it's kinda hard to read this screen but, ah, I think, well, how about four or five hundred dollars, would that be about right?"

How would you feel if you were the customer? And how long would it take you to become offensive and assume that the bank was at fault?

Yes, we want numbers-oriented people in most bank positions, and yes, many numbers-oriented people are lacking in certain people skills. But guess what, numbers-oriented people can be educated in how to deal with people. In fact, is there any more impressive person in the bank than that person who can quickly get to the cause of a problem and suggest possible solutions? How do customers feel when their problems are efficiently resolved? Would just having someone who wanted to help be an adequate substitute for someone who was capable as well as courteous?

NEGATIVE, SUSPICIOUS ATTITUDES

Here are the problem employees! Got any people with bad attitudes back in the bowels of your bank? We thought so. Most businesses do, and they are certainly not restricted to banks. Nor are the bankers always found in the back office. We have seen our share of this problem with loan officers, among others. And yet, banks do seem to have more employees in the back office who have negative people skills than at almost any other position.

Let's look at possible explanations since understanding may lead to resolution. In the first place, many auditors and loan review personnel are hired because they are somewhat skeptical by nature. And anyone working in the back office has to be constantly aware of unusual transactions, whether they be numerous deposits that might look like a "kite," unfavorable trends in financial statements, accounts that are difficult to reconcile or unusual activity in an employee's checking account.

In short, the nature of certain bank jobs tends to require suspicious or inquisitive minds. Suspicion and skepticism can slide easily into cynicism with the resulting negative attitude, which is easily seen but hard to define.

So what should we do with someone whose negativity affects not only the customer but the "internal" customer, too?

For starters, if you, the reader, are one of these people, you may either refuse to recognize that your attitude is poor, or you may disagree with those who have mentioned it to you. In either case, one of two things will happen.

1. You will be fired.

2. You will be passed over for promotion.

Either course is detrimental to your career. But good bank management will not allow customers and peers to be long abused without taking action.

Managers should think carefully about how to handle employees with a poor attitude. We are convinced of two things:

1. Many people can change their attitudes.
2. Most of them don't.

In today's customer-driven market there is precious little room for this type of behavior. At the same time we must admit that there is much wrongdoing by customers and bankers alike. A healthy, inquisitive mind-set can be a valuable asset. The key is to temper it with strong interpersonal communication ability that works toward problem resolution, not controversy and consternation. Theodore Roosevelt said: "The most important single ingredient in the formula for success is knowing how to get along with people."

ENTRY-LEVEL EMPLOYEES

Where do we put new employees in a bank? You guessed it, the bookkeeping or filing departments. Why? Because they don't know much. Do we give them adequate training before allowing them customer contact? Are you kidding?

And when we provide training for new employees, what subjects are the most popular? Compliance and procedure. How much time and money is spent on how to handle irate customers, for example? Not nearly enough, we suggest. How much time is spent impressing on new employees the importance of prompt and courteous treatment of the internal customer?

Have you ever been in a situation where the bookkeeping department had a rivalry with the tellers or loan secretaries? Where legitimate requests made by one department or another were ignored or handled carelessly or in an untimely fashion? We've seen this happen time and again. You see, many times the customer contact person simply needs help in order to help the customer. So the back office personnel are effectively one step removed from the psychic income received when a customer has received great service. And yet, the very foundation of a bank's delivery service depends upon fast, accurate information from these areas.

New employees must be taught early and often the importance of the golden rule: Do unto other bank employees as you would have them do unto you.

Enough about the negative. Let's talk about specific instances in which back office personnel can make positive contributions to the sales effort.

BE SUPPORTIVE OF A SALES CULTURE

From top management down to your supervisor, people with whom you work are dependent upon you to deliver consistent, quality service. They ask you to do one or more of the following:

- Attend training sessions.
- Smile when speaking on the phone or personally to customers and other employees.
- Keep a positive attitude.
- Read this book (we hope).
- Be conscientious and accurate.
- Be supportive during sales meetings.
- Don't be envious of other employees who may have a different pay structure from yours.

There are a couple of very good reasons why you should pay attention to the items listed above:

1. It's your job.
2. You may be on the front line or part of management yourself someday.

The sales staff in today's banks may or may not have as strong a technical background as you. Your job is to teach them, not to be rude and discourteous. Your ability to defuse customer complaints, to make a customer feel good about a problem even when the fault was theirs, makes it possible for customer contact people to enhance customer relationships, instead of having to be defensive when a customer complains to them about "your dummies" in bookkeeping, or the trust account that is constantly out of balance.

BE A TELEPHONE GENIUS

Can you imagine what banking would be like without the telephone? Neither can we. Certainly your job of handling customer inquiries and complaints would be much different. But the telephone requires certain essential skills if it is to be converted to a sales instrument. Here are our helpful hints:

1. Answer the phone as if your best customer or your boss were on the other end. Would this change your attitude?
2. Smile before you pick up the phone. If smiling is a problem for you, get a mirror and put it in front of you (this is a serious suggestion; it works).
3. Get a tape recorder and tape yourself on the phone. Play it back to see how you really come across to the customer.
4. Answer the phone this way: "Bookkeeping department, this is Betty"; "Trust department, James speaking"; "Good morning, this is Sue Jones."

Stating your first or entire name will:

- Prevent a customer from having to ask;
- Speed up the call;
- Personalize the call (you are a person, not a thing); and
- Create an attitude that may decrease hostility or increase likelihood of a sale.

5. Listen, listen, listen. Let the irate caller vent pent-up frustrations. Show empathy and understanding.
6. Repeat what you have heard to let your customer know that you understand the situation.

7. Use pacing, that is, try to talk at the same tempo as the caller.
8. If it becomes necessary to put someone on hold, ask the caller's permission first. Then check back often; don't just leave the caller on hold.
9. Always remember that your goal is to satisfy the customer. In so doing, an opportunity to help might present itself.

For example, assume that a customer calls the bookkeeping department inquiring about a returned check. Under certain circumstances, a suggestion that the customer consider applying for an overdraft protection checking account might be appropriate.

SUMMARY

Many bank employees have little or no external customer contact except by phone. Nevertheless, by doing their jobs right, these bankers can prevent customer dissatisfaction to begin with. And then, if a customer can be converted from dissatisfied to satisfied, loyalty may be enhanced. We don't usually think of sales skills as a requirement for back office jobs, but they are important and can be learned. The internal and external customer both depend upon the back office to provide the foundation of superior customer service.

CHAPTER 13

Putting It All Together

Thank you for getting this far. Now let's tie this entire strategy together. In this chapter we'll review the information previously presented and reinforce the major concepts.

WHY SELLING?

Throughout this book we have emphasized our concept of selling as helping. We sincerely believe that bankers from the newly hired bookkeeping clerk to the chairman of the board are involved in this business to help people. As our friend at Louisiana State University, Dr. Willie Staats, so eloquently points out, the goal of a bank is to enhance shareholder wealth. We believe that we can best enhance shareholder wealth by providing superior service and help to the customer. We believe that service is and can be a sales strategy. We hope that we have made our case strongly enough that you will agree with us.

In our opinion, there will continue to be a demand for outstanding community bankers. We define outstanding bankers as those who are customer-driven, willing to revamp to a sales culture, and forward-looking enough to hire and train talented people. The excellent banker of the future will overcome the negative image of the pushy salesman and redefine sales as the professional career it should be.

OVERCOMING BUILT-IN RESISTANCE

Remember the banker's mind-set we discussed in the first chapter:

1. We have products and services that are different and scarce and our role is to ration them among those who want them.
2. Salespeople are unprofessional and pushy as personified by the offensive used car salesman; therefore, selling is something we consciously and subconsciously do not want to do.
3. We can provide additional services to our customers if we can get the legislative and regulatory approval to provide such services and products as insurance, real estate, securities, etc.
4. We have a long-term, special relationship with our customers, and our desire is to enhance that relationship and attract new customers to a similar relationship.

Do you agree with us when we assert that most bank products and services are no longer unique? Can you now believe that "professional salesperson" is not an oxymoron?

Will you consider getting involved with your state and national associations to remove restrictions from offering other products and services? We believe that the banking industry from a regulatory standpoint may be about to undergo structural change not seen in at least 50 years. The ability to compete in other areas should be part of that change.

As far as our fourth assumption is concerned, we continue to agree with the notion that bankers are and want to be relationship oriented. We have tried to convince you that relationships are built on and dependent on the selling/helping process. In other words there is no conflict between selling and relationship enhancement. The authors of the book *Bankers Who Sell* put it this way: "Banking's new objective of relationship banking presents another powerful argument in favor of building a personal selling program."

WHY NOT SELLING?

In Chapter 2 we stated the reasons why bankers weren't sales-oriented. The problem starts at the top and change must begin there. We related the stories of the lack of training, the lack of CEO involvement, the need for change due to competition, deregulation and technology. And we acknowledged that many of us got into banking so we wouldn't have to sell. We believe that bank culture must be sales-oriented in order to survive. To quote from *Bankers Who Sell*:

> "With a strong sales culture, everything involved in the selling program is easier; without it, genuine progress in developing a sales program is virtually impossible."

The authors then proceed to list six characteristics of a sales culture.

1. Customer orientation: We've referred to this as marketing or customer-driven.
2. Pervasive selling attitude: Everyone in the organization must believe in the culture of selling.
3. Sense of "team": One of the most valuable side effects of the change should be a sense of teamwork. Many of our bank examples relate how teams have competed and worked together.
4. Institutional pride: The opportunity for everyone to own a piece of the sales program and to buy into the mission statement creates pride in the banks.
5. Visible top management commitment: Throughout this book and throughout our consulting and training programs, we emphasize this point. The survey developed by the authors identified lack of management commitment as the biggest problem in any sales program.
6. Faith in employees: Only through the employees can the help be given.

THE PROCESS OF HELPING

In Chapters 3 through 7 we laid out five steps in the process of selling/helping:

1. Prospecting
2. Identifying needs
3. Presenting
4. Handling objections
5. Gaining commitment

Our major emphasis was on how to deal with existing customers. We attempted to take the apprehension out of the process by showing first how to expand current relationships through needs analysis, a process sometimes called "qualifying." Our emphasis was on building trust and rapport with the customer and then discovering the customer's needs. The secret to this part of the process had to do with the art of asking pertinent questions. Not until the process of needs identification was complete could the banker make the presentation.

In the presentation stage the banker was encouraged to get feedback along the way so as to minimize objections from the customer. The idea of helping the customer should prevent bankers from offering a product or service to a customer that would not meet the customer's needs. Integrity in the selling process is essential for two reasons: First, we are bankers and must always maintain high standards and, second, the relationship is always more important than the transaction.

The sales process both culminates and, at the same time, begins when the customer makes a commitment. It culminates in the sense that the transaction is consummated. It begins in the sense that service after the sale is what builds and maintains relationships over time.

WHO IS THE SALES FORCE?

By now it should be evident that our belief is that every bank employee including the janitor and security guard is in sales because they are involved in helping customers. We've attempted to outline the specific steps that each group should take. In Chapters 8 through 12 we gave you some specific ways that five groups could be involved in the selling process. And one of the overriding goals was the formation and enhancement of relationships. Let's look at the importance of relationships to customers as well as bankers.

WHY CUSTOMERS WANT RELATIONSHIPS

Obviously, what customers want from banks depends upon their own unique needs. A business wants availability of credit. Yet, according to a survey of small businesses taken in late 1990 by a trade association, National Small Businesses United, some 91 percent of small businesses feel that they are facing a credit crunch. More than half of them who recently applied for expansion credit were turned down. Businesses want not only availability but consistency. They want to deal with the same loan officer for more than six months at a time. This is where community banks can excel. Businesses also want quick service from a local source who is knowledgeable about their business, someone with whom they have a relationship.

In an article in RMA's October 1990 *Journal of Commercial Lending*, Steve Cranfill related that some surveyed customers were assigned a new loan officer every 1.8 years. His obvious question: "How can relationships be enhanced with that kind of turnover?" How indeed?

Individuals may want relationships for some of the same reasons already mentioned. Certainly most want relationships where service quality is consistently high. But many people, especially in today's difficult economic climate, want relationships with banks that are perceived as not only prestigious, but safe and sound. They want to feel that one or more bankers know them personally and that their banking business matters to the bank. But, most of all, they want help with their financial affairs.

WHY BANKERS WANT RELATIONSHIPS

Take this simple true/false quiz:

	True	False
1. It takes more time to establish new relationships than to enhance present ones.	_____	_____
2. It costs more to prospect for new business than to keep existing business.	_____	_____
3. There is more risk in dealing with customers where no real relationship exists.	_____	_____
4. There is more profit in relationship banking.	_____	_____
5. In many community banks, there are a limited number of new customers to be found.	_____	_____

If you answered "true" to these questions, then it should be obvious why relationships are important to banks. There is very little, if any franchise value left to banking. We submit that the true value of a bank is in the continuing income stream generated from its strong customer relationships.

The selling strategies we've outlined will work, but only if the leadership comes from the top. The specific steps of selling must be studied, practiced, memorized until they become a part of each and every bank employee.

We've been talking about a process of change. Don't expect miracles in the beginning. The program will evolve and continue to improve if done properly. The desire and ability of each employee to help the customer at all times is what creates the image of a bank with quality service.

In Chapter 15, you'll read how dozens of bankers are putting creative sales ideas into practice. Pick one or two or a few, or better still, design your own products, services and sales strategies. We sincerely wish you the best in your continuing career. The future of banking depends on people like you. We appreciate having had the opportunity to help.

CHAPTER 14

Great Ideas from Our Surveys

This is a very special chapter. Essentially, it is a gift from just a few of the wonderful people who have been in our seminar audiences over the last couple of years. Because we believe that most bankers find it easier to emulate someone else than to be totally original, and because we wanted to show that some bankers really are doing creative things in sales, we asked this question on our surveys:

One of the key components in our research is being able to share the good news. In other words, instead of telling so many war stories about how we made bad loan decisions, it is much more positive to be able to say, "This is how the Second National Bank managed to capture new customers, increase profits, become sales oriented, utilize directors in marketing, etc!"

If you have a success story, however small or large, won't you share it with us and give us permission to use it in our book or other training materials? You may use the space below to describe your program or attach another sheet or two or enclose newspaper articles and handouts. Don't be modest!

Want to know the sad part? Less than 10 percent of the participants had anything at all to write about. That, in itself, is instructive. The shortest answer with a twist of humor attached was "Squat."

But here's some good news. You're about to read some of our best answers. We wish we could include them all, but thanks anyway to all who shared their successes.

BOARD IDEAS

"We have appointed a Junior Board of Directors that consists of high school students who are chosen by the schools. Students must apply for the position, and of course we disclose no confidential banking information in the meetings. The students regard being on this board as a very high honor and even the son of a competitor bank president is on the board."

PASCAL HOSCH, EXECUTIVE VICE PRESIDENT
First National Bank
Tulia, Texas

"We are a rural bank, about $25 million in assets. We use 10 percent of profits (we are making $1^{1}/_{2}$ to 2 percent returns on assets) as a bonus for our employees. As a result, we operate with ten employees because they want the bank to earn more so that they can receive a larger bonus. Most banks our size in Kentucky have 15 to 20 employees."

CHARLES W. GATTON, DIRECTOR AND
CHAIRMAN
Sacramento Deposit Bank,
Bremen, Kentucky

"While employed at a previous bank we introduced a 'Lunch with the Banker' program whereby bankers brought two or more prospects to our bank for lunch. We had a chance to visit with prospective customers after giving them a tour of our bank and answering any questions about the banking business. This is a very successful business development tool and we were able to involve our board members in it."

> THOMAS E. KELLEHER, VICE PRESIDENT
> Heritage Bank
> Willmar, Minnesota

"Our bank created a young advisory board made up of young, 'on the way up' successful business people in the community. We did this to groom them to become regular directors in the future and so that they could make contacts with other people of similar age, interest and income levels, etc. Doing this brought many new customers to the bank from a segment of the community that we had been unable to tap in the past."

> R. JEFFERY CANNON, VICE PRESIDENT
> Morris State Bank
> Dublin, Georgia

"As a new director and stockholder, I don't have a success story yet, but I will say that one of the reasons I got involved in the bank as an investment was the ease by which marketing and marketing techniques could be transferred from one retail business to another. In my opinion, the future success in the banking industry will depend on how quickly the industry will adopt these techniques."

> BILL CALHOUN, VICE CHAIRMAN
> Unity National Bank
> Houston, Texas

"We have weekly one-hour employee meetings where we talk about cross-training and bank products. We give customer needs and service the number one priority. All employees are concerned about the bank's future because we have excellent leadership at the board and CEO level. They motivate and are generally concerned about customers as well as employees.

Examples speak very loudly. What's important to senior officers rolls downhill and they enforce our culture. Education mixed with concern and people skills equals unlimited opportunities."

> LINDA FISHER, ASSISTANT VICE PRESIDENT
> National Bank of Andrews
> Andrews, Texas

CEO IDEAS

"During harvest time we have a drawing with the names of our farm customers in a pool. Each of our officers draws a name, contacts that farmer and then puts in one full day of labor for that farmer doing whatever needs to be done. The farmer appreciates that we are willing to get our hands dirty."

> STEVEN L. MICHEL, PRESIDENT AND CEO
> Henderson State Bank
> Henderson, Nebraska

"We brought in good management, restructured and conducted extensive training, in-depth goal-setting classes for everyone, which resulted in tremendously improved self-esteem, self-image and overall professionalism. This resulted in a total bank image change, which translated to improve customer/client relations and ultimately improved profitability— earnings going from a loss of 0.80 ROA this year to projected 1.00 to 1.25 ROA next year. We've doubled our income from 1987 to 1988. We're just completing a merger of a $35 million bank, all of which was possible only because of the extensive training we've done with all our staff."

> STEVEN D. BOGARD, EXECUTIVE VICE PRESIDENT
> Keokuk Savings Bank
> Keokuk, Iowa

"We came up with an idea to sponsor a Knowledge
Fair. This was used to introduce or educate all
employees in all areas of the bank. Each employee was
divided into one of seven teams who rotated between
seven different sessions. Each session was 15 minutes
long with a five-minute break. We met after for snacks
and to answer questions. The areas covered were: (1)
Lending, (2) Data Processing, (3) Operations/
Bookkeepers, (4) Account Representatives/Tellers,
(5) Mortgage Loans, (6) Trust Services. This was well
received by the 70 or so employees."

> JOE VEHSTADT, PRESIDENT
> Bank of Bellevue
> Bellevue, Nebraska

"We feel that we have gained customer loyalty
through explaining to them not only what we are
doing, but why we are doing it, through a very
informal newsletter sent out every two months. Some
banks have a consumer advisory group and we have
one, only we like to think that it consists of 100 percent
of our customer base. Their response to our customer
surveys is outstanding and they care enough to let us
know when there is an occasional time when service is
not up to what they consider to be our usual standard.
Also our bank is an easy bank to manage as our
present employees will not tolerate a new employee
being discourteous or thoughtless in their customer
relations." (See Figure 14.1.)

> ALICE M. DITTMAN, PRESIDENT
> Cornhusker Bank
> Lincoln, Nebraska

"The president of our bank reviews the local
newspaper and personally sends a congratulatory letter
to an individual or his or her parents when someone is
recognized in the newspaper."

> BARB RITZE, CASHIER

Buffalo National Bank
Buffalo, Minnesota

"We are developing a sales contract for employees
and directors as well as a commission structure. We are
looking to hire a person that has 80 percent attitude
and personality and teach the remaining 20 percent
technical. We also have a policy that our employees are
to call each customer by name three times while they
are in the bank. This not only makes the customer feel
good but disciplines us to know our customer better."

BILL MCGAUGHEY, PRESIDENT AND CEO
Nashoba Bank
Memphis, Tennessee

"We had a meeting where we put the president on
trial for not selling bank services. Everyone in the bank
received a summons to appear. We went through all the
new marketing products and how important it was to
cross-sell. It was really funny and made quite an
impression on everyone."

SUSAN FOOSE, ASSISTANT VICE PRESIDENT
Canandaigua National Bank
Canandaigua, New York

"On July 1, 1989, our bank president, who had been
with the bank since May 14, 1919, offered his
resignation from full-time responsibility. At 94 years
old we elected him chairman and created a new
position and gave him an office on the main floor near
the teller line and entrance so that he could meet new
customers and be active in public relations. If a
94-year-old can be sold on being customer-driven,
surely anyone else can as well."

B. G. OWSLEY, PRESIDENT AND CEO
The Cecilian Bank
Cecilia, Kentucky

FIGURE 14.1   Results of Cornhusker Bank Survey

Cornhusker BANK
Member F.D.I.C.

Responses to Questionnaire — 1991

1) Which bank location do you use most?
a) Main Bank Lobby	311	c) North 27th	117	e) Bethany	93	g) South	77
b) Main Drive-In	283	d) North 27th Drive-In	113	f) Bethany Drive-In	78	h) South Drive-In	95

2) Do you think we should consider another location?   Yes **223**   No **608**

3) If you needed to borrow money what would you consider? (Number 1-5 with 1 being most important.)
a) Convenient Location	114	d) Professional attitude	129
b) Dealing with a familiar officer	375	e) Other	23
c) An institution that has the lowest interest rate	455		

4) If you needed to borrow money, would you consider Cornhusker Bank for a (check all applicable):
a) Car Loan	579	e) Credit Card:	MasterCard 119	Visa	184
b) Home Improvement Loan	409	f) Medical or Other Emergencies			310
c) Refinance a Home	226	g) New Home Loan			236
d) Business Loan	308				

5) What is important to you when considering an institution in which to deposit money? (Number 1-5, with 1 being most important.)
a) Convenient Locations	330	f) Government deposit insurance	397
b) Dealing with a familiar staff person	200	g) Strong capital ratio	153
c) Institution with the highest rates	190	h) Lowest service charges	252
d) Professional business attitude	121	i) Knows me by name	108
e) Prompt service	181	j) Other	8

6) What could Cornhusker Bank do to enhance your money management comfort level? (Check three that are most important to you.)
a) Explain how my funds are protected	180	d) Better brochures outlining services	162
b) Seminar on money management	191	e) New Service:	45
c) Spend more time one-on-one with me	146	f) Nothing, fine the way it is	484

7) If a statement were offered that listed your checks by number, but did not include your cancelled checks, would you be interested? This would reduce your service charges.   Yes **203**   No **604**

8) We offer the following accounts. Please check the ones that best meet your needs:
a) Senior Citizen (55 and Over)	304	g) Church and Charitable	27
b) Paper Carrier	18	h) Discount Brokerage	25
c) Savings	478	i) Business Checking	128
d) Full Service Checking Account	674	j) Individual Retirement Account (IRA)	116
e) Certificate of Deposit	341	k) Repurchase Agreement (REPO)	10
f) Money Market	160	l) Tax Deferred Annuities	63

THANK YOU   THANK YOU   THANK YOU   THANK YOU

The responses to almost 1,000 surveys that were returned out of 12,000 mailed are shown above. We very much appreciate your assisting us in guiding our future. We were interested in the responses of approximately ¼ of our customers indicating we should consider another location for their convenience. The numbers showed approximately ⅓ of those designating another location preferred the downtown and southwest area of town. It was especially interesting that most of our customers considered government deposit insurance the most important to them in their decision on choosing a financial institution. We hope they will also find interesting the article on FDIC Insurance on the front of this newsletter. A convenient location was second most important. The third choice, low service charges, is an obvious one, and we have had an excellent record in comparison with other financial institutions in keeping our costs low. We were extremely pleased that the largest number of our customers responded to question number 6 that they liked our bank just the way it is. We can also assure you we are always trying to improve. Question number 7 showed that customers prefer the return of their cancelled checks. You may be sure we will not discontinue this practice; and if a new service is offered, it would be entirely the customer's choice to accept a limited service account.

In question number 4 we were a bit concerned at the low response rate to 4 c and 4g, that our customers did not think of us in financing a home. For all of our existence we have been active in financing homes on farms, acreages, and in all areas of Lincoln and the smaller, surrounding communities. In addition to this, we now have the capability of placing longer term home loans in the secondary market to permit customers to qualify for FHA, VA, NIFA, and conventional 15 and 30 year home mortgages through our 56th & South Branch. Just give us a call and we will direct you to the right person.

We would like to share some of the comments on the surveys returned with you, and a few are as follows:

FAVORABLE RESPONSES TO NEWSLETTER

*"Thanks for the job you are doing."   "We think you do a wonderful job!!"   We are glad you are close and within walking distance."
"Just keep up the friendly, special service."   "You are doing fine." (about 12 of these)   "Thank you for the 56th & South location."
"I am glad I am with this bank."   "You are always fast. I get my statements immediately."   "So far so good."
"Bigger is not always better."   "Friendly, efficient service."   "Friendly, warm and personal."
Everyone treats me nice, and I have been with you many years."   "I have always been treated in a friendly, professional manner."
"Continue to show strong support for the local community."   "Thank you for your concern."   "You are always there when we need you."
"I have had nothing but good experiences at your bank."*

AREAS WE NEED TO IMPROVE:

*"Longer hours."   "Lower service charges."   "Faster service at the Drive-Up."   "Improved statement format." (we are working on this)
"Faster mail service."   "Drop Celsius from your time/temp sign." (already done)*

Source: Alice M. Dittman, president, Cornhusker Bank, Lincoln, Nebraska.

MANAGERS, SUPERVISORS AND LENDERS

"We are located near a college and on registration day we open new accounts and hand out student loan applications. After graduation many of the young people stay with us."

ROSE MARY HOUCK, BRANCH MANAGER
First American Bank
Gallatin, Tennessee

"A woman walked into our bank and asked a manager to use the rest room. She was dressed 'less than average' but was pointed in the right direction. She left the bank and returned very shortly with a $100,000 cashiers check drawn on the bank across the street. Her comment was that her old bank would not permit her to use *their* rest room, so now our bank was her bank."

BRADLEY T. HOOVER, VICE PRESIDENT
The First Tennessee Bank
Kingsport, Tennessee

"We hold a luncheon every other Friday. Each officer or key employee can invite customers or non-customers for lunch. Everyone has a chance to meet new people in the community which raises the bank's visibility."

LEAH ANN MADEWELL, LOAN ADMINISTRATOR
First State Bank of Denton
Denton, Texas

"We use a Master AG Note. Once it's set up, the borrower then only has to borrow what he needs when he needs it. They no longer have to drive to the bank to sign a note each time. They can call in advance."

DAVID A. EICKHOFF, PRESIDENT
The Adrian State Bank
Adrian, Minnesota

"During the 1989 planning process, in the fall of 1988, The New Iberia Bank decided to place some emphasis on the consumer loan market. Traditionally, the Bank had primarily been commercial oriented and had not actively pursued the consumer market. 1989 was the year to change that mind-set. In January 1989, the Banking Services division was born. The Main Office New Accounts/Customer Service area, the BankCard/Overdraft Protection area and the Installment Loan area were rearranged and put in the same location of the Bank. This area began remaining open each day from 9:00 A.M.–5:30 P.M. and until 6:00 P.M. on Fridays. Teller transactions are handled here, also. The Installment Loan area began to actively seek indirect dealer loans. Through a clever advertising campaign, and by asking customers and the entire bank staff to refer business, the walk-in and referral traffic dramatically increased. December 1988 Installment Loan portfolio was $7,651,239; December 1989 Installment Loan portfolio was $14,465,444. One year, new attitudes and a definite direction made The New Iberia Bank Banking Services division a success story."

> GINGER LAURENT, ASSISTANT VICE PRESIDENT
> The New Iberia Bank
> New Iberia, Louisiana

"Many of our loan originators were reluctant to sell and market. We received a call asking someone from our bank to help put on an instructional seminar for Realtors. We created a class designed and approved for continuing education credit for Realtors and that gave us lots of market visibility for our bank and an opportunity for our loan originators to meet new Realtors. It provided for the Realtors, a chance to have an open discussion with our lenders as well as giving them credit toward maintaining their licenses."

> CAROL HOUSE, LIAISON/MARKETING DIRECTOR
> Norwest Banks
> Billings, Montana

"We have begun a service quality sales program that involves every employee in the bank. It does not include directors at this time. Each person has a quota of contacts to make over a specific period. Incentives range from silver coins to a trip to Hawaii for two. The goal is to increase all types of accounts in our bank with particular emphasis on different areas each quarter. We expect this program to fundamentally change the way we do business forever."

RICHARD E. CATHEY, SENIOR VICE PRESIDENT
First Commerce Bank
Commerce, Georgia

"We were interested in increasing consumer loans so we introduced a pre-approved loan program. The forms were mailed to the customers and generated immediate new loan volume. After 18 months we have no delinquency problems."

HAROLD K. SULLIVAN, VICE PRESIDENT
First State Bank
Greenville, Kentucky

"You can't be afraid to 'ask for the business' and be successful in today's sales culture. I've used many opportunities to offer loans to people and some respond immediately, others when the need arises. For example, a small MasterCard or auto loan approval gives you an opportunity to see someone's financial position and credit. If they have equity and other debt, I call and offer a home equity loan to consolidate other debt and put it on a tax deductible loan. Even if they don't respond immediately, when they need something they remember who called them and offered them money. Always look for cross-selling opportunities."

JOHN L. MILLS, ASSISTANT VICE PRESIDENT
Norstar Bank
Utica, New York

"In the past we have viewed our neighboring banks as the enemy. We recently contacted two of them that had strong loan demand and went to visit them and asked them for their overline loans. Rather than them selling their overlines to large correspondent banks, we were able to increase our loan portfolio by three million. The key was to assure those banks that we were not going to steal their customers, rather help them in serving that customer."

> Joe Sindelar, President
> First National Bank
> Schuyler, Nebraska

"At one of our affiliated banks we were known as the 'little bank in town'; many people were unaware of us and our products until we became involved in indirect financing to increase our consumer loans. We held a Mini-Auto Show directed at increasing community awareness of us and enhancing our relationship with the auto dealers. We ran ads, had a raffle, and offered a special rate. The program met our business goals."

> Pamela K. Stefik, Assistant Vice President
> First National Bank of Blue Island
> Blue Island, Illinois

Our marketing program is part of our five-year continually updated strategic plan. We have an annual planning retreat for all officers and our marketing plan is coordinated with the annual operating budget. We get total participation from all managers, do our best to hire great people and pay them well so that we can maintain them. We also have one of the most successful senior citizen programs in the country which we call 'The Overton Park Bluebonnets'."

> Lou Wooten, Executive Vice President
> Overton Park National Bank
> Fort Worth, Texas

"We are giving away free TVs with every car loan. When the member returns to their office carrying a small TV it really starts them to talking the credit union up. It has generated excitement among our membership and creates lots of good feedback."

> LOUISA MAXSON, ASSISTANT VICE PRESIDENT
> Texas Health Department Credit Union
> Austin, Texas

"Since loan officers have the best opportunity to sell, and since most borrowers borrow more than they actually need, the closing of the loan offers a perfect time for the officer to sell bank services. The bottom of our loan closing checklist is a listing of all the services our bank offers. Loan officers should have picked up on any of the services that could be sold to the customer during the loan interview. Many times we have had the customers take the loan check, cash it at the teller line, then open a special account because of the loan officer's suggestion. Normally they may have cashed the check and just walked out the door."

> JAMES C. DAVIDSON, LOAN OFFICER
> First National Bank
> Manchester, Kentucky

"While making a very modest $3,500 loan to a long-standing, small-loan customer, I decided to simply ask for his deposit business, expecting a very small DDA account. Imaging my surprise when the customer moved $125,000 to our bank and the reason given: I had asked for his business."

> MARY JO HILL, LOAN OFFICER
> Monroe County Bank
> Forsyth, Georgia

"Officer turnover, though undesirable, is sometimes unavoidable. We managed to keep almost all of our customers because the senior lending officer wrote to each significant customer a letter telling them who their new loan officer was. The new officer then followed up with a phone call and a visit to those customers, introduced him or herself and got to know the customer."

> DIANE MCCARTNEY, VICE PRESIDENT
> Promenade National Bank
> Richardson, Texas

CUSTOMER CONTACT

"A pre-approved VISA or MasterCard program is offered to indirect car loan customers who have been approved for a loan. A postcard reply is enclosed with the letter of offer. When current installment loan customers call the bank to find out how much interest has been paid for the prior year, they are asked if they are a homeowner. If they are, we send them information on the home equity line of credit with a letter which begins, 'INB is looking out for your best interest.'"

> SUSIE ESSIG MOORE, LOAN OFFICER
> INB National Bank
> Lafayette, Indiana

"We conduct a customer service interview with customers who have opened an account or moved their business. This interview policy allows us the opportunity to try to salvage good accounts and expand new relationships."

> ELIZABETH BROMBACH, ASSISTANT VICE
> PRESIDENT
> St. Anthony Park State Bank
> St. Paul, Minnesota

"We established Advantage Checking, a service charge free, no minimum balance checking account. We also allow unlimited check writing. However, we require truncation of all checks and also require that the customer use duplicate checks. This will enhance his ability to keep his balance. The check numbers are posted on the statement making a cross reference to his check stub easily discernable. As of this past month (October 1990) we have opened 1,100 accounts since 1988. There were approximately 18,000 checks posted to these accounts and the average balance maintained in these accounts has been averaging approximately $380 to $400 per month. This has produced a maintenance-free, low-postage-cost account and we have, due to an excellent Customer Service Representative, had phenomenal success that has given us something for low to moderate income people as well as others—absolutely no problems and no complaints.

"We also offer no service charges on our regular accounts as long as the balance is maintained above $400. The point is our Advantage Checking Accounts are averaging close to and sometimes over $400 and we don't have to file 18,000 checks (at this time) or check off 18,000 checks on bank statements, and do not have to provide postage to mail the checks except for the bank statement only. We only allow personal and private accounts. No business, commercial, etc."

> BARRY ARMSTRONG, PRESIDENT
> Peoples Bank
> Mt. Washington, Kentucky

"One of my Customer Service Representatives recently waited on a customer who complained of an overdraft and a returned check. After discovering the customer was a senior citizen who did not deposit his social security directly in our bank, our CSR was able to sell a direct deposit, a new retiree checking account with overdraft line, and a credit card. Her problem-solving ability was the key to this success story."

> DENNIS A. HAGGERTY, BRANCH MANAGER

Norstar Bank of Upstate New York
West Winfield, New York

"We recently completed a several-week class that met for two hours a week and provided education for our new accounts people. We taught them all about the products and how to call. The classes ended with each taking a non-customer to lunch. Two of the four got the customer's entire account relationships. We intend to start the tellers on this program next month."

MARK E. BAKER, ASSISTANT VICE PRESIDENT
Citizens Fidelity Bank, Madison County
Richmond, Kentucky

"We feel the key to our success is by recognizing each customer by name, thanking them for their business and making them feel extremely welcome and appreciated. We try to be more than a bank by providing all types of financial services to our community. We are still the only bank in town with an automated teller machine."

JOSEPH JONES, PRESIDENT
Merchants and Planters Bank
Bolivar, Tennessee

"Our success is due to our recent hiring of personnel who are sales oriented. We are a small community bank and personalized attention has enabled us to increase profits dramatically while restructuring our balance sheet and increasing our outstanding loans."

WAYNE M. TURNER, SENIOR VICE PRESIDENT
First Commercial Bank
Bradenton, Florida

"In our drive-in facilities we started giving out dog biscuits to all customers with their pet in their cars. The customers love it and their dogs can't wait to get to the window."

TODD TUTT, ASSISTANT VICE PRESIDENT
American State Bank
Lubbock, Texas

BancFirst, an Oklahoma bank with 14 branches, enjoys a solid reputation as a customer-oriented bank. Their commitment to quality service was recently evidenced in their extensive training program in which we have assisted.

Each level, from the teller, CSR/CSO to the lending officers/presidents will participate in in-depth product knowledge, customer service, management and sales training.

After a minimum of 21 hours of classroom work, tellers and CSRs participate in a graduation ceremony and an exciting recognition day. Their CSO and president attend, lunch is served and a plaque given to each graduate. The graduates also receive, for the first time, business cards.

After graduation they are eligible to participate in BancFirst's incentive program. Unlike many incentive programs, the bank rewards for *asking* a customer for business, even if nothing new is sold. Their Request and Refer program builds self-confidence and rewards for asking. The goal, of course, is to increase business and build long-term client relationships in a consultative way.

Lorri Porter of the Stillwater Bank had a recent success with this program. She sent a letter to a customer telling him of a service that could save him money. (See Figure 14.2.) The customer responded with delighted surprise and eventually business resulted (See Figures 14.3 and 14.4).

The Request and Refer program has been eagerly embraced even though there was initial trepidation. Front line and platform people were concerned that asking customers questions about their needs would be perceived as being too aggressive. Their attitude now is one of consultative problem solver. The customer can't be helped unless asked about their needs. *Then* it can be determined how BancFirst can best be of assistance.

FIGURE 14.2   Sample Letter from Request and Refer Program

*Banc*First

808 South Main
Post Office Box 1
Stillwater, Oklahoma 74076-0001
Telephone 405/372-3133

November 20, 1990

Dear Roger:

It has been quite some time since I visited with you concerning your account and other accounts we have to offer. I thought it might be helpful to restate some of the information we discussed.

In reviewing your account, I noticed you have been making several withdrawals from your account — which results in a high service charge. I hope that I can be of assistance in reminding you that BancFirst offers a "BancFirst" checking account. I have enclosed a brochure which shows the details of the "BancFirst" checking versus the "Basic" checking (which you currently hold).

If the "BancFirst" checking account looks appealing or you have other questions, please feel free to contact me.

We appreciate your business.

Sincerely,

Lorri L. Porter,
Customer Service Representative

Reprinted with permission.

FIGURE 14.3   Sample Response from Request and Refer Program

---

24 November 1990

Lorri L. Porter
Customer Service Representative
BancFirst
808 South Main
P.O. Box 1
Stillwater, OK 74076-3133

Dear Lorri,

Thank you very much for your reminder about changing checking
accounts from the low transaction to the unlimited transaction.
I, too, reviewed my account, and unless I am misreading it, I am
still paying less per month in service charges than I would flat
monthly fees for the unlimited transaction account.

If I am in error, please contact me so that I may reconsider
which checking account is more appropriate to my needs.

Again I thank you very much for showing so much concern for such
a lowly little account. I'm not sure who to thank, you
personally or BancFirst's policies, but I am a very happy
customer.

Sincerely,

Roger

Reprinted with permission.

FIGURE 14.4   Follow-Up Letter from Request and Refer Program

___

*Banc*First

808 South Main
Post Office Box 1
Stillwater, Oklahoma 74076-0001
Telephone 405/372-3133

November 28, 1990

Dear Roger:

Thank you for the kind letter. I have enclosed a print-out which breaks down the service charges of the Basic checking and the BancFirst checking accounts.

If you believe that you will be making less than 15 withdrawals per statement cycle, the Basic checking is the account you want to stay in. However, if you plan on making 15 or more withdrawals per statement cycle, the BancFirst checking would be a good option, having a lower service charge.

I hope that the enclosure will explain in more detail. Again thanks for the kind words.

Sincerely,

Lorri L. Porter,
Customer Service Representative

___

Reprinted with permission.

BACK OFFICE

"We recently ordered business cards for each member of the bank's staff including tellers and bookkeepers. It is not only a morale booster, it has helped bring in business."

> WALTER MCCRARY, JR., PRESIDENT
> First State Bank of Randolph County
> Cuthbert, Georgia

"The one service that really indicates our dedication to our customers is our willingness to call customers when they have an overdraft. We pay our good customers and give most of the marginal ones a chance to cover their checks before the daily deadline. All customers appreciate this service and it has created many referrals for us, not because we call on overdrafts, but because we are perceived as a good service provider. We waive probably 10 percent of charges and feel more than justified in getting $17.50 per check if we call."

> JOHN STEVENSON, VICE PRESIDENT
> Citizens National Bank
> Victoria, Texas

"Thirty of our employees on a volunteer basis are working on an Adopt-A-School program in cooperation with the Fort Worth Independent School District. We adopted Northside High School, a predominantly Hispanic school. Some of our employees act as tutors, others as counselors. The students are taken on field trips to our bank and other businesses and many of these students have been given part-time jobs that have led to full-time positions with our bank."

> KEN NOEL, VICE PRESIDENT
> North Fort Worth Bank
> Fort Worth, Texas

PROMOTIONS/CONTESTS

"We introduced a new Club Account. To promote the account we held an eight-week contest with two teams. The team captains were non-officers. Points were given for each new account signed up with non-contact personnel given twice as many points per account. Each Friday became a 'theme' day with dress-up and decorations. The contest promoted camaraderie and team work, selling, and the morale of the bank improved. The local newspaper took photographs—free advertising. At the end of the contest we sponsored a dinner. The losers of the contest served the winners steak and the losers had beans. We gave gag awards and ribbons were given to the winning teams and prizes to the top sales people. Seven hundred fifty new accounts were signed up in eight weeks, but the morale boost was even better. Have you ever seen the president of a bank in a clown suit or dressed up like a nerd?"

PATTI COOPER, MARKETING OFFICER
Security National Bank and Trust Company
Duncan, Oklahoma

"We had a new accounts contest which raised over $12 million in deposits. The winner, as a grand prize, won a week in Hawaii."

BOBBY ATCHLEY, LOAN REVIEW OFFICER
Texas Bank
Weatherford, Texas

"We took the money that had already been budgeted for radio and newspaper advertising and used it to give scholarships for graduating seniors in our county. The bank's image and visibility grew as a result."

MARK ESTES, SENIOR VICE PRESIDENT
West Texas State Bank
Snyder, Texas

"We had a beach party kickoff for a new checking account we were offering. We had food, gave prizes. Everyone dressed beach-style. The fun time generated almost 100 percent employee participation in selling the new account."

> KEVIN ROTH, ASSISTANT VICE PRESIDENT
> Grabill Bank
> Grabill, Indiana

"We offer low-interest Christmas loans to customers with the proviso that the monies be spent in our community. The merchants pay a discount on 'Christmas Bucks' when they are deposited with the bank. Consumers shopped in town, sales went up for the retailers and the goodwill the bank gained was tremendous. Also, to date no delinquencies."

> DOROTHY CRANFORD, REAL ESTATE OFFICER
> First Madison Valley Bank
> Ennis, Montana

INCENTIVE IDEAS

"We had an excess of empty safe deposit boxes so we gave employees one day off for each ten lock boxes they sold. It worked very well."

> MAX HAIN, VICE PRESIDENT
> First National Bank
> Quitaque, Texas

"We have made the educational process fun. We created teams to play 'football' games on a weekly basis. Answering questions correctly about our products allows the team to move the ball to score. The winning team wins cash. Every employee from the president to the custodian is involved. We have become far more knowledgeable and have had great fun."

> LOUIS PRICHARD, VICE PRESIDENT
> Farmers National Bank of Danville
> Danville, Kentucky

"We publish a sales force newsletter recognizing the sales efforts of all employees."

> BETH DOWDAKIN, STAFF AUDITOR
> First National Bank of Rockford
> Rockford, Illinois

"A 'shopper program' was instituted and each employee who receives a 'good shop' got $10. The money is passed out by the president or a senior vice president each Friday afternoon. To get a good shop, the employee (officer) need only do the following: (1) smile, make eye contact with the customer, (2) call the customer by name during the transaction, (3) be courteous and helpful to the customer, (4) thank the customer for their business. It helped morale and customers perceive us as more friendly."

> ALLAN SHIELDS, PRESIDENT
> Alamo Bank of Texas
> Alamo, Texas

"We give incentives in the form of movie passes, money, candy and lunches to all employees who are observed by officers and directors promoting the bank when out in public. We also have a secret call-in person who, if told by our employee, 'Thank you for letting us help you,' can reward the employee with $10. Needless to say, our employees are good at remembering the 'magic phrase.'"

> DORIS HOURIGAN, LOAN REVIEW
> American National Bank
> Wichita Falls, Texas

"A prior bank employer had a fish bowl of silver dollars and a fish bowl of all employees names. Management would ask the employee whose name was drawn from the fish bowl a question concerning customer service, bank products and the accounts which are offered at that bank. If the employee at the bank gave the correct answer they would get a chance to go to the bowl of silver dollars and get out as many silver dollars as one hand could pull out. Good morale and a good way to increase knowledge of bank products offered."

JUDITH A. KEALLY, VICE PRESIDENT
First National Bank
Fairfield, Texas

"We pay commissions on credit life and accident and health insurance sales and we also pay commissions on new real estate loans that are solicited by officers. Incentives work."

CHARLES P. WILSON, PRESIDENT
McKenzie Banking Company
McKenzie, Tennessee

"We have begun a 'Phantom Sales Force,' a voluntary program open to all employees with no additional compensation. The employee receives basic training from the marketing department and is rewarded by recognition for each sale. At the end of each month a list of services sold and the Phantom Seller who sold them is given to the president. He writes a personal letter praising the individual for their sales performance. He also gives a report to the board on Phantom Sales. The reward is strictly recognition which, of course, will be converted later into promotions for those employees. It has been very successful."

GLENDA TOLSON, VICE PRESIDENT
Simmons First National Bank
Pine Bluff, Arkansas

"We have had for about 45 years, an incentive compensation program for commercial lending officers in addition to the base salary. The interesting thing is that the commission percentages of new money have been gradually weighted more heavily toward new customers as opposed to new loans to present customers. This has helped by providing a gradual move to a sales and marketing environment."

TIM SHARP, ASSISTANT ACCOUNT EXECUTIVE
Midwest Commerce Bank
Elkhart, Indiana

MISCELLANEOUS

"We developed Extra Effort advertising program to communicate 'We go the extra mile for you.' It also raised employee morale and productivity.

"Looking for new ways to meet customer needs, SNB implemented the program 'Just Call Jane,' encouraging customers to call with problems, questions, suggestions.

"A referral/sales program for Customer Service Representatives and Personal Bankers includes training incentives, recognition and rewards.

"We've developed a program to recognize and reward employees at all levels for performing service excellence. The program features include the PRIDE award, recognition and monetary rewards for employee suggestions."

LISA WILSON, MARKETING DIRECTOR
Security National Bank
Sioux City, Iowa

"We opened a branch in a food store with Thursday and Friday hours until 8:00 P.M. and all day Saturday. By telemarketing and door-to-door calling we met our first-year goal in the first six weeks of operation."

JUDY SNEED, BRANCH MANAGER
Sovran Bank
Chattanooga, Tennessee

"We use Dun and Bradstreet business research cards to prospect for SBA loans, with great success."

> BEVERLY MCJILTON, SBA LOANS
> First State Bank of Cleburne
> Cleburne, Texas

"Because we (individuals) recognized the need to develop good, effective skills, a core of bank officers set up our Toastmasters Club. After participating for about a year our Senior Management recognized the improvement in speaking skills. They asked us to organize a speaker's bureau for the public schools. Anticipating a mild response, we did. What happened was that we have given as many as six presentations a week. The benefits were: (1) we continue to improve public speaking skills, (2) we pass on valuable information to students, also several have opened savings accounts, and (3) their parents have thanked us and in some cases moved to our bank. It is my opinion that future benefits will even outweigh the current. I base this on the fact that the kids have an exposure to Credit/Banking/Savings."

> BRENDA ALLRED, OPERATIONS OFFICER
> First National Bank of DAC
> Las Cruces, New Mexico

"I was previously in a branch management capacity. Near the office was a retirement home. Many of the residents were near invalid and had a difficult time getting to their bank. Our idea was to go to the home a couple of hours a week for very basis services, cash some checks, change orders, etc. The residents were very happy, and business began to grow. We began going more often and even rented a room for a permanent office offering all services. A branch is now located there with a vault and security system. We also now have branches located in every major retirement home, obtaining a large source of deposits, particularly

CDs. We saw such a lucrative market in the over-50 age
market, and created a new product—Access 55—
offering many services tied to a free checking account
to anyone over 55 years old. Aggressive deposit goals
were set for the first year, and a marketing plan was
developed. All goals were shattered in the first few
months, getting several million dollars in DDA
accounts, and many CDs. Loans also grew considerably
during this period. Star Bank now has an image of
being a bank for the retail side, when we were
primarily attributed to being a commercial bank just a
year before."

> TIM VANDERHORST, CORRESPONDENT BANKING
> Star Bank, Cincinnati
> Cincinnati, Ohio

"We set up a project called 'Project Up North.'
When someone new is moving to the community,
Realtors inform the bank. The bank sends the
prospective newcomer a subscription from the local
paper along with a welcoming letter and a request for
accounts. This has worked well for us."

> REED CAMPBELL, BRANCH MANAGER
> The First American Bank
> Brainerd, Minnesota

"We send flowers to funerals and to each customer
who is in the hospital."

> ANITA WYNNE, LOAN REVIEW OFFICER
> Farmers State Bank
> Groesbeck, Texas

"We have a $20 unconditional guarantee, 'If for any
reason you are unhappy with the service at Vistar
Bank, tell us—we'll fix it and give you $20.'"

> JULIE SVOBODA, VICE PRESIDENT

> Vistar Bank
> Lincoln, Nebraska

"We host a summer conference for our borrowers at local resorts. Participants include the families of the customers and bank employees. Three days of activities for all ages are planned which results in excellent marketing opportunities."

> MARK NOBLE, ACCOUNT REPRESENTATIVE
> Cobank
> Columbia, South Carolina

"Lake Oconec is a new Georgia Power Lake in Greene County. By making sales calls on as many new residents as possible in the lake area, we have increased deposits and loans for our bank. All you need to do is *ask* for the business. Also, our bank is very active in recruiting new businesses for Greene County which is growing tremendously because of the lake. Far-sighted thinking pays off!"

> KATHY TOPKEN, LOAN OFFICER
> Bank of Greensboro
> Greensboro, Georgia

"We have been involved with the Georgia Bankers Association's 'PEP' (Personal Economics Program) and have found that it has helped in attracting new loan customers through deposit accounts and making personal contacts. We are happy with the results and have found that this had helped the bottom line from both directions."

> MICHAEL A. MORRIS, LOAN OFFICER
> Bank of Greensboro
> Greensboro, Georgia

"A previous bank I was with sponsored a 'Senior Citizens Day,' which consisted of renting the local movie theater, showing a double feature of the movies that were popular in their day. We served free popcorn and cokes and charged a 25-cent admission. This enabled the bank to get a lot of publicity and we had personnel on hand to answer the questions and open new accounts on the spot. It was a great success."

> KAREN TUTOR, LOAN OFFICER
> Henderson County Bank
> Jackson, Tennessee

"While I was a bank examiner in North Carolina, I notice that the North Carolina National Bank took the attitude when the community reinvestment act became effective, of 'who's going to make money out of this.' They then proceeded to finance the clearing of slums and the revitalization of Charlotte. They gained all sorts of publicity and a great deal of profit. This is an example of turning a difficult situation into a success story."

> GENE EWING, EXECUTIVE VICE PRESIDENT
> First National Bank
> Ballinger, Texas

"We have started a new service called Lifetime Banking. We attempt to handle or assist with all of our customers' financial needs, whether it be investing, insurance, retirement, wealth management or budgeting. We will meet with the customer at their home or office. We will pick up their banking business at their convenience and handle it for them if they are unable to come to the bank. This has been very well received, especially by our older customers."

> SCOTT L. POLLOCK, FINANCIAL SERVICES OFFICER
> INB National Bank N.W.
> Lafayette, Indiana

"We have instituted a new account program to reach new employees at Delco Electronics, Chrysler

Corporation and Cabot Corporation, the major
employers in Kokomo, Indiana. All three are focusing
their future work force on high-tech research and
development. We made contact with the personnel
department at each location and supplied them with
promotional pieces that allow new employees to obtain
free checking accounts and a detailed map of Kokomo.
The new employee gets this kit when they first arrive in
town for training, relocation or introduction to the
company. We have access to employees before they even
finish college or move, depending on the circumstances.
This has a subtle positive effect on the personnel
department itself, and from time to time we have
enclosed a free sample (a coupon worth $5 is added to
the customer's initial deposit)."

> DONALD G. SMITH, MARKETING DIRECTOR
> Central National Bank
> Russiaville, Indiana

"Prospect calls and customer calls result in 40
percent of new business. Referrals account for 30
percent of our new business and telephone calls to
customers or prospects account for the balance. No
new good business walks in the door so prospecting is
essential."

> B. M. RAY, III, SENIOR VICE PRESIDENT
> American Bank
> Corpus Christi, Texas

"In our bank employees are 'associates,' customers
are 'clients' and branches are 'offices.' The largest
shareholder of the bank is our own ESOP.
Consequently, each associate has a strong interest in
providing value-added service. We have a highly
sales-oriented culture within our bank."

> JAY R. CARLSON, VICE PRESIDENT
> Signal Bank, Inc.
> West St. Paul, Minnesota

CHAPTER 15

Ideas from Other Sources

Over the past two or three years we have kept a file on the kinds of programs that successful banks have instituted around the country. Some of this information has come from individuals who sent information at our request, but the majority of it has come from various trade publications and other sources. The purpose of this chapter is to continue the type of information that was found in the previous chapter in hopes that the readers of this book will get additional value by seeing how other banks are doing it.

VERMONT SALES PROGRAM

Last year, Dennis met Muriel Sedergren, vice president of Woodstock National Bank in Woodstock, Vermont, at a seminar on the campus at Dartmouth. As is the case in most sales programs and sales cultures, the program in her bank, EX-SEL, is in a state of evolution. It originally began as a program for CSRs designed to provide incentives based upon their cross-sell ratio, but has shifted emphasis as it developed, to the total customer relationship and the amount of deposits generated. Additional amounts are paid depending upon whether the account represents new money or comes from an outside referral. They have a tracking system on which the CSR marks the services that are sold plus any other services that the customer presently has with the bank. This way the future needs of the customer are also identified since the form clearly shows what services are not presently being used. Most of the reports are prepared for payroll purposes and the results, along with appropriate checks, are shared in a format that guarantees recognition for outstanding performance. Twice monthly, training sessions are held to improve sales techniques and to maintain a high level of product knowledge. They have developed a very organized product portfolio broken into the following groups:

- Transaction Group
- Savings Group
- Investment Group
- Credit Group
- Special Services Group

Each product that the bank offers has a product summary followed by a brochure on the product, followed by benefit statements which the employee can use to help the customer identify benefits. These are followed by a profile of the prospective customers most likely to use the product. Following the profile are need clues, which may represent selling opportunities. In addition, typical objections and responses that a customer might have if they do not buy are listed followed by recommended ways to overcome those objections. Obviously, each of the services is well explained, but typed at the bottom of the product sheet is the name and extension number of the individual in the bank who is most knowledgeable on the service. This program is being broadened to include calling officers and others and has a potential to make a significant difference in the income and client relationships of this banking group.

TOP MANAGEMENT ON SALES CULTURE

According to Donald B. Summers, senior vice president of Rainier National Bank in Seattle and Chairman of the American Bankers Association's Human Resources Executive Committee, "The first step a chief executive officer should take is to send a message that the company is going to be and needs to be sales-oriented." According to Bruce D. Stuckey, senior vice president, Connecticut National Bank, Hartford, Connecticut, "A clear message from the top can be very powerful, but executives should not underestimate the sheer amount of work and energy that needs to go on to support that directional statement." Summers also indicated that not every employee will have the skills or want to make the change.

Gary DeFrange, president and chief executive of First Interstate Bank, Englewood, Colorado, indicated that it was also important to measure progress. The switch to a sales culture will not happen overnight, he indicated, but specific goals should be set and reviewed each year.

These remarks were included in an *ABA Bankers Weekly* article dated December 13, 1988.

WAYS TO INCREASE FEE INCOME

According to the December 26, 1990, *The Wall Street Journal*, many banks around the country are expected to be under pressure to raise fees. According to that article, Citicorp is raising fees on many of its miscellaneous services by 25 percent or more. The article quotes Edward Furash, a bank consultant from Washington, D.C., as indicating that banks will be under much more pressure from 1991 on to raise fee income. According to Sheshunoff and Company of Austin, Texas, banks' net interest margin has declined 9.8 percent in the five years ending 1989, while non-interest income gained 34 percent. But even that may have been exaggerated since much of that fee income was for leveraged buy-out loan fees. One of the objectives Citibank is hoping to accomplish is to encourage more customers to have linked, multiple accounts. Chemical Bank Corporation has also raised its fees recently, but the article strongly pointed out that raising fees above what the customer perceives is fair can be a way to encourage a good client relationship to find a new home.

TAKE IT TO THE CUSTOMER

The First National Bank of Amarillo, Texas, is in the process of refurbishing an English double-decker bus that it purchased several years ago as a promotional tool to take civic groups to destinations in the city. The bus will be outfitted with an automated teller machine, teller stations and customer service counselors who will provide a full range of banking services. The bank has been very creative thanks to its marketing officer Jerry Polvado. This represents only one in a long line of innovative ways to increase customer service. In May of 1990 The First National Bank of Jackson, Tennessee, announced its plans to take its new mobile branch into nursing homes, factory sites, and public housing projects. Their plan is to convert an armored car into a mobile branch.

The First Citizens Bank and Trust Company of Raleigh, North Carolina, now has a mobile automated teller machine embedded in the side of a van. Apparently it will not accept deposits or loan payments, but will travel to fairs and other large gatherings to dispense cash to customers who are ATM clients.

PERFORMANCE PAY

In the May 2, 1989, issue of *ABA Bankers Weekly*, a significant amount of space was devoted to a program developed by W. B. Abernathy and Associates of Memphis, Tennessee. The company developed a checklist to determine how ready, willing and able a bank is to initiate and maintain a successful incentive pay plan. (See Figure 15.1).

WE'LL PAY YOU TO MOVE YOUR BUSINESS

In the summer of 1989, Texas Commerce Bank in Texas began a two week promotion entitled "OnePlus Banking" in which they offered customers $50 to move their business to TCB. Billed as the "most intense retail promotion in the bank's history," the money is to be paid to accounts in good standing

FIGURE 15.1 Checklist for Successful Incentive Pay Plan

Ready

1. Do you know what your organization's culture is?
2. Do you know what you want it to be?
3. Do you have an automated system?
4. Can you easily calculate incentive earnings and produce an incentive payroll?
5. Is there an easy way to track people as they move from job to job?
6. Are there internal people with the skills needed to update the plan?
7. Is there a way to train new internal experts once the original ones move on?

Willing

8. Are you willing to pay top performers 10 percent to 30 percent more than others?
9. Are you willing to provide recognition as well as money?
10. Are you willing to pay incentives biweekly or monthly?
11. Are you willing to let supervisors or workers provide input into their incentive plans?
12. Are you willing to put managers and supervisors on incentives first?
13. Are you willing to train supervisors in the new management skills they will need?
14. Are you willing to commit to a long-term funding strategy?
15. Are you willing to turn future merit increases into incentive opportunity?
16. Are you willing to audit the system?
17. Are you willing to face the new issues?

six months after the transaction and will be taxed to the customer as interest.

FIGURE 15.1   Checklist for Successful Incentive Pay Plan (continued)

Able

18. Are you able to measure and reward individual performance?
19. Are you able to set hourly goals?
20. Are you able to measure all the job (quantity and quality)?
21. Are you able to collect base data?
22. Are you able to quantify the value of quality improvements?
23. Are you able to restructure jobs?
24. Are you able to set global measures for jobs (profitably)?

Source: W.B. Abernathy and Associates, Memphis, Tennessee.

OLDER AMERICANS LIKE CONVENIENCE

In late 1989, Total Research Corporation of Princeton, New Jersey, released a study showing that Americans 65 and older are exhibiting a pronounced preference for convenience, which is characterized by such things as extended banking hours including weekends, the ability to use other financial institutions' ATMs and branch locations near work. Their proprietary research methodology is known as "predictive segmentation" and they believe that it improves market segmentation studies by better isolating the needs and desires of various groups of consumers.

MAKING OFFICER CALLS

One of the most difficult things for many officers to do is to make calls outside the bank. Michael R. Chy, president of Personal Motivation Institute, Inc., Matteson, Illinois, says that making the outside call would probably be a success if you could come away from the initial call with the following information:

- Business name
- Address
- Phone
- When business began
- Number of current employees
- Turnover rate
- Type of industry or profession
- Main office location
- Local decision maker
- Local contact
- Main office decision makers
- Main office contact
- Major products
- Gross sales
- Profitability
- Who do they sell to
- Who do they buy from
- Future plans
- Current services used at other banks
- Primary bank
- Non-bank services used
- Financial related needs or problems
- Main trade publication
- Best product or service ideas for follow-up

Seldom is it possible to get a relationship on the first call, but Michael Chy has given an excellent checklist of information to be gained from that call that would be very valuable in getting the customer's business in the future.

STAR SEARCH

According to the *ABA Bankers Weekly* in May 1989, Frances Flood, vice president and retail director of sales at Star Bank in Cincinnati, Ohio, believes that there are two key ingredients in developing a sales culture—employees and commitment. Star Bank tries to hire people who have not only basic skills but the propensity for a banking career. They hold special sales events, campaigns and incentive programs to improve employee morale. They conducted a "star search rally," wherein Star bankers competed against one another as singers and performers. Employees at Star Bank were awarded points in five areas: deposits and loans, quality service, sales production, training and profitability. Their emphasis was on tracking, rewarding and recognizing performers. The results were higher employee satisfaction and excellent customer service.

STAY ON THE RIGHT TRACK

Wachovia Bank and Trust Company in Winston-Salem, North Carolina, developed a tracking system to help assess sales incentive plans by tracking employee referrals. According to a 1988 survey by *Bank Marketing Magazine*, the biggest disincentives to sales-referral programs of a financial institution are a lack of management backing and poor tracking procedures. Wachovia Bank and Trust calls their system First Wachovia's Account and Tracking System, and it is designed to motivate employees and increase referral participation, which can help improve overall sales results. This program was reported in the April 18, 1989 issue of *ABA Bankers Weekly*.

Sales Quotient Audit

One of the most important tasks facing a financial institution in the next few months is to change into a more aggressive sales organization. To focus attention on the various activities that must be considered in bringing about this change, a series of questions is presented that will be of help in assessing the present sales sophistication of an organization. Readers will want to rate their own organization on each of the following questions from one ("Not True of My Institution") to five ("True of My Institution").

	Not True of My Institution				True of My Institution
1. The organization emphasizes the importance of selling from the top to bottom. The majority of staff members recognize the importance of sales to the future of the organization.	1	2	3	4	5
2. Senior officers of the line divisions (i.e., lending, retail, corporate,	1	2	3	4	5

	Not True of My Institution			True of My Institution	

correspondent, trust, etc.) are accountable for sales results.

3. Within the organization, there is a department or individual responsible for developing and implementing sales strategy.

    1   2   3   4   5

4. Every customer contact person has a sales or customer relations statement as part of his or her job description.

    1   2   3   4   5

5. Lending officers, branch managers, trust officers and others are involved in a sales call program on prospects as well as customers. The program is producing meaningful results.

    1   2   3   4   5

6. The organization has an ongoing sales training program.

    1   2   3   4   5

7. The organization has developed a program for selling segmented customer groups (e.g., via a personal or executive banking depart-

    1   2   3   4   5

	Not True of My Institution			True of My Institution

ment). These personnel, through aggressive selling techniques, are calling on attorneys, physicians and other centers of influence.

8. The organization is developing a product line, priced and packaged competitively, to meet the customers' needs in the Nineties.

   1 2 3 4 5

9. The organization is taking specific steps to provide sales support to line personnel (e.g., the development of a central information file, packaging of products, creative pricing, sales brochures, etc.).

   1 2 3 4 5

10. Cash bonuses and incentives are used regularly as a means of recognition for personnel who achieve sales quotas.

    1 2 3 4 5

11. Outstanding sales performance is an important criterion for promotion to higher levels.

    1 2 3 4 5

	Not True of My Institution			True of My Institution	
12. Primary customer contact personnel, such as tellers, new account representatives and customer service representatives, are trained in sales and customer relations and are measured regularly in these areas.	1	2	3	4	5

A perfect score would be 60 points ($12 \times 5 = 60$). If the results measured 50–60 points, the organization probably has a well-developed sales culture. There may be areas in need of attention, but for the most part, the organization is moving in the right direction. A score of 40–50 points indicates that there is some movement toward the sales culture, but no doubt many areas need immediate attention. The organization is probably not seriously committed at the senior level. Unless change takes place soon, the organization may have problems in the marketplace in the next five years. A score of below 40 points reflects an organization unprepared for the challenging times ahead. There is little if any sales commitment at the senior level, and even the most basic sales programs have not been started or are operating below acceptable levels. This organization will likely not be a winner in the marketplace unless there is dramatic change soon.

Sales Quotient Audit ©Financial Shares Corporation, Chicago. Reprinted with permission.

Bibliography

Albrecht, Karl, and Ron Zemke. *Service America*. Dow Jones-Irwin, 1985.

Alessandra, Wexler and Barrera. *Non-Manipulative Selling*. Prentice Hall Press, 1987.

Berry, Bennett and Brown. *Service Quality*. Richard D. Irwin, Inc., 1989.

Berry, Futrell and Bowers. *Bankers Who Sell*. Dow Jones-Irwin, 1985.

Berry, Leonard, and Donna Massey Kantak. *Selling in Banking: Today's Reality, Tomorrow's Opportunity*. 1988.

Donnelly, Berry and Thompson. *Marketing Financial Services*. Dow Jones-Irwin, 1985.

Donnelly, James Jr., and Steven J. Skinner. *The New Banker*. Dow Jones-Irwin, 1989.

Drucker, Peter F. *Managing in Turbulent Times*. Harper & Row, 1980.

LeBoeuf, Michael. *How To Win Customers and Keep Them For Life*. G. P. Putnam's Sons, 1987.

McCuistion, Dennis. *The Prevention and Collection of Problem Loans*. Bank Administration Institute, 1988.

McCuistion, Niki. *Excellence and Quality in Customer Service*. 1982.

Norman, Thom, and Niki McCuistion. *Telephone Marketing: Prospecting and Obtaining Appointments for Greater Success in Selling*. 1987.

Office of the Comptroller of the Currency. *The Director's Book*. 1987.

Peters, Tom. *Thriving On Chaos*. Alfred A. Knopf, 1987.

Willingham, Ron. *The Best Seller*. Sales Communications, Ltd., 1984.

Wright, Don. *Bank Marketing for the 90s: New Ideas from 55 of the Best Marketers in Banking*. John Wiley and Sons, 1991.

Index